One Minute after EVERY MILE
running the race

Jo Anna Rieger

WESTBOW
PRESS®
A DIVISION OF THOMAS NELSON
& ZONDERVAN

Copyright © 2016 Jo Anna Rieger

All rights reserved. No part of this book may be used or reproduced by any means, graphic, electronic, or mechanical, including photocopying, recording, taping or by any information storage retrieval system without the written permission of the author except in the case of brief quotations embodied in critical articles and reviews.

All scripture, unless otherwise indicated, taken from the Holy Bible, NEW INTERNATIONAL VERSION®. Copyright © 1973, 1978, 1984 by Biblica Us, Inc. All rights reserved worldwide. Used by permission. NEW INTERNATIONAL VERSION® and NIV® are registered trademarks of Biblica Us, Inc. Use of either trademark for the offering of goods or services requires the prior written consent of Biblica US, Inc.

Scripture quotations from The Message, copyright © by Eugene H. Peterson 1993, 1994, 1995, 1996, 2000, 2001, 2002. Used by permission of NavPress Publishing Group.

Scripture quotations from The Holy Bible, English Standard Version® (ESV®), copyright © 2001 by Crossway, a publishing ministry of Good News Publishers. Used by permission. All rights reserved.

Scripture taken from the Contemporary English Version © 1991, 1992, 1995 by American Bible Society, Used by Permission.

This book is a work of non-fiction. Unless otherwise noted, the author and the publisher make no explicit guarantees as to the accuracy of the information contained in this book and in some cases, names of people and places have been altered to protect their privacy.

WestBow Press books may be ordered through booksellers or by contacting:

WestBow Press
A Division of Thomas Nelson & Zondervan
1663 Liberty Drive
Bloomington, IN 47403
www.westbowpress.com
1 (866) 928-1240

Because of the dynamic nature of the Internet, any web addresses or links contained in this book may have changed since publication and may no longer be valid. The views expressed in this work are solely those of the author and do not necessarily reflect the views of the publisher, and the publisher hereby disclaims any responsibility for them.

ISBN: 978-1-5127-2915-3 (sc)
ISBN: 978-1-5127-2917-7 (hc)
ISBN: 978-1-5127-2916-0 (e)

Library of Congress Control Number: 2016901703

Print information available on the last page.

WestBow Press rev. date: 03/25/2016

Contents

Preface ix
Acknowledgments xiii
Introduction xvii
Chapter 1   Start 1
Chapter 2   Train 14
Chapter 3   Breath 26
Chapter 4   Heal 39
Chapter 5   Pace 49
Chapter 6   Gear 61
Chapter 7   Race 79
Chapter 8   Recover 91
Chapter 9   Finish 111
Notes 137

This book is dedicated to Deborah A. Robinson.
You inspired many to run "the race" well.

Whom have I in heaven but you?
And earth has nothing I desire besides you.
My flesh and my heart may fail,
but God is the strength of my heart
and my portion forever.
—Psalm 73:25-26

Preface

This book is the result of a series of challenges—a rollover car wreck, job change, miscarriage, physical injury, home renovation, and the death of a dear friend. In the midst of these challenges I signed up to run a half marathon. Shortly after running this race, my school year ended, leaving another year of teaching behind. By this time my entire being was left numb, broken, and worn. My husband encouraged me to go away and rest. I did. I dedicated much of my time to hours of journaling. The hours added up to days. The days moved on to weeks. I simply followed a voice that told me to write. Words continued to fill pages as the weeks turned into months, forming the book you now hold.

The book's underlying theme is running. The race mentality is something many understand and have understood for thousands of years. Driving down the road today, you will probably see a car decal such as 5K, 13.1, or 26.2. The numbers on these decals stand for the distance of the race a runner has accomplished:

- 5K = 5 kilometers (3.106 miles)
- 13.1 = half marathon of 21.097 kilometers (13.109 miles)
- 26.2 = full marathon of 42.195 kilometers (26.219 miles)
- 50 = shortest ultra-marathon of 50 kilometers (31.07 miles)

One that has never run a race may wonder what it takes to actually cross the finish line. Preparation involves all aspects of the runner. Their mind-set is as important as physical skill, training, gear, and nutrition. A runner plans, stays calm, focuses on his or her goal, and perseveres. Upon crossing the finish line, the runner reflects on the race. He or she takes in what went well and what can be changed for the next time.

This book was birthed out of reflecting on the annual Door County Half Marathon.[1] *One Minute after Every Mile* was actually a concept I learned at this race. I signed up for the race with the mind-set of beating my last half-marathon pace. An injury and running the race with my friend Jane changed this goal. Prior to this race, rest was not a part of my definition of persevering. In fact, it seemed counterintuitive. Perseverance is staying power, continuing on. Rest comes after a race, not during it.

I was wrong. Perseverance and rest go hand in hand. I ran this race with Jane, and we walked an entire minute after every mile we ran. The principle of walking one minute after every mile actually ensures restoration. It creates a stint of breath and refocuses the runner. It allows for hydration. This one minute of rest supports a strong, injury-free run for every mile after.[2]

And it did. I ran the race, soaking in the beauty of early spring. I persevered, strong to the end without injury, and was left with a book full of life's lessons.

My desperate need for margin was exposed by this race. Richard Swenson defines margin as "the space that once existed between us and our limits. It's something held in reserve for contingencies or unanticipated situations. Overload is not having time to finish the book you're reading. Margin is having time to read it twice. Overload is fatigue. Margin is energy. Overload is red ink. Margin is black ink. Overload is hurry. Margin is calm. Overload is anxiety. Margin is security. Overload is the disease of our time. Margin is the cure."[3]

Since that race, walking one minute after every mile has become a profound metaphor for the benefits of purposeful rest while running in the race of life. My athletic life had always paralleled my daily life, pushing through no matter how I felt until I met my goal. This left me exhausted and angry. God was calling me to lie down, to sit at his feet, and to give up my burden. He wanted to teach me how to *really* run this race on earth.

For forty years, I ran life's race my way. I rejected the Sabbath—a time for surrender, restoration, and refocus. I worked in my own strength, leaving me frustrated and drained. Much of my example of how to live came from church. Sadly, many church organizations have replaced their first love, being God, with busyness, buildings, and programs. Oswald Chambers stated that "the greatest competitor of devotion to Jesus is service for him."[4]

Distractions and cluttered agendas are Satan's way of blocking a Christ follower from living a life that glorifies God.

If we desire to run well, all the way to our heavenly finish line, we need a *spiritual race mentality*. We cannot leave life's race up to chance. Diversions and clutter must be pushed aside to bring a focus on our goal. We need to adopt a radical plan that includes specific disciplines. *One Minute after Every Mile* will provide insight into running our spiritual race well. My prayer is to see you strong at the finish line!

Acknowledgments

This book exists because of the support and encouragement from many individuals. Matt Rieger, my husband, has been literally running with me for the last twenty years. We are also partners in *life's race*. Matt gives love generously and knows how to boost my spirit. His smile heals. His touch calms. His validations bring hope to carry on. It was his encouragement to go away and rest that provided the margin to write this book. The name Matthew means "gift of the Lord"—this he is.

Although Matt and I go way back, Dennis and Geri were there from the beginning and are still two of my biggest fans. My parents' sacrifice ensured that I had an education and resources to become the woman I am today. I would have never taken on a book project without the work ethic and organization skills Dad taught me. Mom exposed me to God's Word at a young age. This exposure laid the foundation for the life I now live in Christ. Without my parents, this book would not exist.

And then I have my "sisters." They stick close, listen to my stories, speak truth, and pray with me. Throughout the day I receive blessings and encouragement. If I am in crisis, they are there serving. I never do life alone. A few of their stories are shared in this book.

I have been privileged to sit under amazing spiritual teachers. These teachers followed their calls, stayed the course, and presented God's Word without apology. I have a shelf of Bibles full of notes from their sermons. My journals reflect on their teachings. This book is the natural overflow of their years of faithfulness.

No race would have been run without the vision of David Elliot and Lars Johnson, the co-founders of the Door County Half Marathon. The Peninsula Pulse, which dedicated an entire page to advertise the Door County Half Marathon, was also crucial for sparking my interest in this race. Countless hours were volunteered by many for the success of this race. It was an amazing event, and continues to be, because of these folks.

Kathy Navis has spent hours assisting in my healing. I was led to her yoga studio shortly after running the race written about in this book. In my brokenness, she taught me how to be still, breathe, and fully engage in the moment.

Annie Hall signed up for my women's small group while working in the Chicagoland area. We were hooked up as accountability partners during her four-month stay. Our precious time during this short season built a forever friendship. One of our many adventures is touched upon in this book. Annie was the first set of eyes to read *One Minute after Every Mile*. Her encouragement and support persuaded me to pursue sharing it with others.

Marty Erickson is not only my "sister" and colleague at work, but also the one who dedicated hours to making sure the message of *One Minute after Every Mile* was clear, powerful, and true. Marty had her work cut out—I am trained as a visual artist, not a writer. She graciously offered suggestions and was never condescending. Her thoughtful questioning and subtle ideas brought new life to this book.

Peggy Fox, my former colleague and research specialist, assisted in the technicalities of this book. She is another gracious individual who gave of her time, assuring the authenticity of this book's contents.

Julie Kresl was the last set of eyes to read this book prior to my pursuit of publishing. Julie and I began teaching together in 1996. We became friends and began to study Scripture. Julie gave her life to Jesus Christ not long after. Since then, Julie has been a constant source of biblical sharpening. She was up in Door County the day of the half marathon that inspired this book. She encouraged me to write.

Miriam Martin kept me well fed and nurtured during the final stretch of publishing preparations. Her keen eye, sensitive heart, and love for Christ brought this book to its close. I am blessed to call Miriam my new neighbor.

And lastly, my thanks goes out to the great team I worked with at WestBow Press. Taking on a publishing project is no small task. My publishing team offered patience, guidance, and expertise each step of the way.

Thank you.

Introduction

> Do everything without grumbling or arguing …
> as you hold firmly to the word of life.
> And then I will be able to boast on the day of Christ
> that I did not run or labor in vain.
> —Philippians 2:14, 16

The race. My favorite biblical metaphor for living life. *One Minute after Every Mile* holds the formula for what goes into this race. What race, you ask? The race one signs up for when becoming a disciple of Jesus Christ. This race is no sprint. It is a long-distance run, traveling through many seasons, demanding intentionality.

From dietary blogs to juicing documentaries, hours can be spent researching health and fitness trends. Many athletes' budgets include health club memberships, organic diets, or massages. Signing up for a race will require sacrifice and the dedication of even more resources. Do we, as Christ-followers, exert the same amount of effort when training for our spiritual race, the race that ends at heaven's door? Do we worry about having the proper gear, techniques, and strategies? Do we understand that our race in life ends at the foot of our Judge and Maker?

This book is for Christians who are serious about running "the race" well and are ready to meet God with no regrets. Scripture and story are intertwined to demonstrate what this race could look like. Christian authors provide an abundant amount of resources. However, God's Word is where the power to change lies and should never be substituted for the words of a book. As you read *One Minute after Every Mile*, pause each time you encounter Scripture. Reread it. Let it sink in. Ask yourself what God wants you to grasp from it. God's Word should always be your *main* guide for running well.

All Scripture is God-breathed and is useful for teaching, rebuking, correcting, and training in righteousness.
—2 Timothy 3:16

One Minute after Every Mile is not only the title of this book but a phrase that has stuck in my head since running my first Door County Half Marathon. It is a way of life that guards my health and stops me in my tracks. It is the red warning light that flashes in an overheated car. In the middle of a jam-packed, nonstop day, just at the point of "overheating," my conscience screams, *"Stop! It's been way over a mile!"* This reminder brings my focus back to the race of life I am in, the finish line I am aiming for, and what needs to happen to make it there in a way that pleases our Lord. Regular overheating, exhaustion, and burnout are not found in God's plan for a successful race.

Those who live according to the flesh have their minds set on what the flesh desires; but those who live in accordance with the Spirit have their minds set on what the Spirit desires. The mind governed by the flesh is death, but the mind governed by the Spirit is life and peace.
—Romans 8:5–6

The body, mind, and spirit are all part of "the race," each one dependent on the other. In order to run well, the health of each must be considered. Getting through this book is *not* a race. Each chapter of this book ends with a segment titled "Stop and Abide." Recovery is a must in any run or prolonged pursuit. "Stop and Abide" is meant for pause, reflection, and healing of the body, mind, and spirit. Sit here as long as you need to do. Margin is a gracious gift to give yourself and others. Giving yourself space promotes restoration, allowing you to minister to others in a more effective way.

"Stop and Abide" begins with a section labeled "Relax." This section attends to your body, focusing on simple techniques to aid in physical healing. Conscious engagement with these simple techniques will force the body to slow down. Do not skip "Relax." The body is intertwined with the mind and spirit. Bringing attention to the body directly affects all other aspects of who we are.

"Reflect" is the next section. It focuses on the mind. Questions and passages are provided as a place to start this reflection. These may be bypassed for another Scripture or concept from the chapter into which you want to dig deeper. Here is your space to do so.

Lines are provided for writing, but you may choose to use your own journal. Do not replace writing with a conversation in your head. Writing is a form of healing. It forces the mind to slow down, allowing the heart to catch up, and creates a record to return to.

The "Eyes Up" section appeals to the spirit by offering a poetic prayer that encompasses the struggles detailed in the chapter. Let the words be a catalyst for your own prayer, carried to the foot of God's throne. Sit, kneel, or lie down—whatever posture brings you to a humble realization of going before the King of Kings and Lord of Lords. Confess your sin by filling in whatever comes after *ashamed of*. Worship our God by beginning with *you are* statements. Pour out many thanks, listing what you have been *blessed by*. Let your requests be made known with a plea of *please*.

One Minute after Every Mile is not meant to be read for pleasure. It requires honest reflection. Its goal is to challenge the way you are running your race. No more status quo. Force yourself to turn off life. Allow the words of Scripture to penetrate. It might take waking up well before dawn, skipping your lunch break, or finding a corner to hide in late at night. It may mean fasting from social media, television, or the Internet. The world is loud. Fight back and secure a quiet place to allow the Holy Spirit to speak and expose what needs to change. If this sounds like hard work, I cannot lie—it is. But, rest is in sight, your reward will be great, and you are never alone while running life's race!

1

Start

> Therefore, since we are surrounded
> by such a great cloud of witnesses,
> let us throw off everything that hinders
> and the sin that so easily entangles.
> And let us run with perseverance
> the race marked out for us,
> fixing our eyes on Jesus,
> the pioneer and perfecter of faith.
> —Hebrews 12:1–2a

A recent study claimed extreme runners suffer heart damage after an intense race.[1] The study focused on ultra-marathoners—runners who exert themselves for extremely long durations at maximum speed. Are you feeling pretty good about the five-mile run you accomplished today? An ultra-marathoner can run two marathons and a 10K daily.[2] That is fifty-three miles in addition to the five-mile warm-up you accomplished. These runners commit to run as many races in a month as life allows. This kind of pace offers little time for recovery.

We do not have to look hard in today's world to find that we are surrounded by "ultra-marathoners." No, I am not talking about athletes who are up before dawn, getting in their thirty miles before the start of their day. I am talking about the workplace ultra-marathoners. These are the workaholics, ultra-disciplined, 100 percent reliable, hardworking, and conscientious people who struggle with taking a vacation. I used to see these labels as compliments. They are anything but compliments. Without balance, these labels are arrows for demise. I know because my life has often reflected that of an ultra-marathoner—week after week, month after month, year after year, running a grueling pace without rest.

Our pace gets set in childhood. Parents or other close adults in life act as coaches. Our pace is often set by our "coaches'" expectations, words of affirmation, and modeling. Hard work, perseverance, and performance—these were the words "coaches" planted in my head as a young child. I assumed *rest* was a word for the weak or lazy. Extreme efforts birthed personal pride, with a habit of people-pleasing.

Although we faithfully attended a fundamental Bible church, Sabbath, a day of rest, was an ancient biblical term never practiced. Our day of worship became one of the busiest days of the week. We knew the following verses well, yet never applied them to our family.

By the seventh day God had finished the work he had been doing; so on the seventh day he rested from all his work.
—Genesis 2:2

This is what the Lord commanded: Tomorrow is to be a day of Sabbath rest, a holy Sabbath to the Lord.
—Exodus 16:23a

There remains, then, a Sabbath-rest for the people of God; for anyone who enters God's rest also rests from their works, just as God did from his. Let us, therefore, make every effort to enter that rest, so that no one will perish by following their example of disobedience.
—Hebrews 4:9–11

Our family thrived on busyness. We ran a tight weekly schedule that included music lessons, church events, family gatherings, chores, and schoolwork. Holidays were full of elaborate preparations. Vacations centered on what we were going to do instead of how we were going to rest.

This pace will wear down even the most vibrant child. During one of our busy seasons, my parents contacted the police to file a missing person's report. I was the missing person, only a toddler at this point. Fortunately, just hours later, I was found sleeping soundly on a bed of freshly fluffed towels in the dryer. This was a desperate cry for rest in a home that never stopped.

As I grew up, so did the demands. My teen years added landscaping jobs, babysitting, and assisting aging grandparents. I joined track, pompoms, band, and choir. I served as an Awana leader, joined the worship music team, was labeled the church artist, and became a student leader in our high school youth group. I had a booming social life, yet remained in the top ten of my class by spending the only time I could find in my day to get homework done—while the rest of the world slept.

College pushed my performance to another level. Extracurricular activities shadowed the same intense schedule I followed in high school. I also began working as a house cleaner and nanny. I immediately secured a teaching job upon graduation that included K–12 art, junior-high math, and adult ESL. After six months I began working on a graduate degree. I continued to serve in multiple roles at our small church. This insane pace continued much the same for another eighteen years—until I was *made* to "lie down."

> The Lord is my shepherd, I lack nothing.
> He makes me lie down in green pastures,
> he leads me beside quiet waters,
> he refreshes my soul. He guides me along
> the right paths for his name's sake.
> Even though I walk through the darkest valley,
> I will fear no evil, for you are with me;
> your rod and your staff, they comfort me.
> You prepare a table before me
> in the presence of my enemies.
> You anoint my head with oil; my cup overflows.
> Surely your goodness and love
> will follow me all the days of my life,
> and I will dwell in the house of the Lord forever.
> —Psalm 23:1–6

My control panel lit up, flashing with every warning available. I was blind. I did not see the havoc I was wreaking on my heart by the busy life I led. Being *made to* lie down is painful. A good shepherd will not tolerate a sheep that continues to go astray. He may break its leg, forcing it to lie down and depend on him for care. Ironically, this forced method of becoming dependent instills a trust and love for the shepherd. God used this same process to get to the heart of an ultra-marathoner.

I was *made to* lie down during my fortieth year of life, a milestone year that made its mark. It was a year that forced refocus and rest. This was all in God's plan. But why did he let me go all the way to forty before getting my attention? Maybe he had been getting my attention all along, but my rebellion dismissed his calling. No matter what, God's way and timing are always perfect.

Forty is a significant number with many references to it throughout literature and life. I enjoyed seeing how this number was used in the Bible and the parallels it had to my own life:

Forty in the Bible

Rain fell on the earth 40 days and 40 nights.
—Genesis 7:12

Moses entered the cloud as he went up on the mountain and he stayed on the mountain 40 days and 40 nights.
—Exodus 24:18

The Lord's anger burned against Israel and he made them wander in the wilderness 40 years.
>—Numbers 32:13

A judge must not impose more than 40 lashes.
>—Deuteronomy 25:3

The land had peace for 40 years.
>—Judges 3:11

For 40 days [Goliath] came forward every morning and evening and took his stand.
>—1 Samuel 17:16

David rested with his ancestors and was buried in the City of David. He had reigned 40 years over Israel.
>—1 Kings 2:10–11

Solomon reigned in Jerusalem over all Israel 40 years.
>—1 Kings 11:42

So [Elijah] got up and ate and drank. Strengthened by that food, he traveled 40 days and 40 nights.
>—1 Kings 19:8

Jonah began by going a day's journey into the city, proclaiming, "40 more days and Nineveh will be overthrown."
>—Jonah 3:4

After fasting 40 days and 40 nights, [Jesus] was hungry.
>—Matthew 4:2

After his suffering, he presented himself to them and gave many convincing proofs that he was alive. [Jesus] appeared to them over a period of 40 days and spoke about the kingdom of God.
—Acts 1:3

Turning forty pushed me into a new decade of life known as "over the hill." I had reached the summit and now was headed back down the hill. I have hiked many mountains. There is a pause that comes from enjoying the accomplishment and surroundings from making it to the top. And then, the descent begins. It involves a completely new perspective from what was seen and felt going up. It is easier than going up and takes half the time. My fortieth year forced me to see life from a new perspective.

Throughout that year, I experienced a number of events that exposed the "damage" incurred from running a pace without allowing recovery. My ultra-marathon way of life had left me tired and numb. Yet, I do not feel that my life is very different from many of the other people with whom I do life. How many other Christians are "running" at an ultra-marathon pace? Have they begun to feel the effects too? I regularly hear that my friends are adding more and more to their plates, forcing them to work harder and longer to keep up with life. Rest seems like a dream only the lucky enjoy. So many Christians long to be Mary, sitting at Jesus's feet, yet they also want to run wildly like Martha. When rest is in sight, another giant responsibility lands on their plate. Is this the hand with which some were meant to deal? Or is it the pace at which some choose to run life?

> As Jesus and his disciples were on their way, he came to a village where a woman named Martha opened her home to him. She had a sister called Mary, who sat at the Lord's feet listening to what he said. But Martha was distracted by all the preparations that had to be made. She came to him and asked, "Lord, don't you care that my sister has left me to do the work by myself? Tell her to help me!"
>
> "Martha, Martha," the Lord answered, "you are worried and upset about many things, but few things are needed—or indeed only one. Mary has chosen what is better, and it will not be taken away from her."
>
> —Luke 10:38–42

Did Martha have a choice to leave her busy agenda behind? Of course she did. When we give up our agenda for God's agenda, we will find ourselves sitting at Jesus's feet, as Mary did. Regularly sitting as Jesus's feet ensures a run that is strong to the finish. This is what Martha was missing. She kept holding on to what she thought she had to do to serve Jesus. Holding on to her own agenda was robbing Martha of the abundant life Jesus had for her. She was choosing desert living. What Martha could not see was that restoration from desert living comes from letting go and looking up, from trusting and surrendering to God.

It was a lack of trust and surrender that kept the Israelites from entering the Promised Land. When we run the race of life without trust and surrender, we set ourselves up for desert living. Just like the Israelites, I wandered in the desert for forty years, clinging to what I thought I had to do. At forty, God made it clear that I could leave desert living behind by trusting him with my life, knowing he was in control and that he wanted the best for me. I would need to surrender my schedule, timeline, to-do list, goals, and desires. This trust and surrender would offer the abundant life Jesus promised. This is a description of *running* well.

Only recently did I make the connection between life and running. My love for running began freshman year at Timothy Christian High School. It was 1989. My main events were the 800-meter relay and one-mile run. It was during this season that I learned the strategies for long-distance pacing and endurance. This experience was the beginning of a lifelong discipline of exercise and has kept me running ever since.

My husband, Matt, and I purposely bought a home that sits between two Rails to Trails[3] paths. We run on them regularly. These trails produce an escape from the busyness of life. Most of the trails are lined with trees and are home to a wide variety of animals. Other parts of the trails are surrounded by thick woods, ponds, and prairie. The trails go on for miles and miles. For the last twelve years, these trails have not only served as the training ground for each race I run, but they also create a place to restore.

Allowing for a healing of our bodies, restoration for our hearts, and a recentering on God are essentials for running strong through life's race. We must purposefully attend to our physical, emotional, and spiritual beings. This takes time and a deliberate turning off of daily life—concepts that are often foreign in today's world. The frenzied pace of our Western culture is the opposite of meditation. Patience has long left America. Our reliance on the Internet and smartphones creates a desire for "I want it now!" We are instant–gratification addicts. We rarely shut down. Phone alerts sound throughout the night. Daytime planners are packed for weeks. Relationships have moved to a virtual realm. How long can our culture sustain this? Even more important, how long can the church sustain this? What kind of damage has been done due to this extreme way of life?

This is the perfect place to pause. You need time to stop and refresh. It takes discipline to do so. Do not jump over the last portion of this chapter or any chapter that follows. It is a place designed for healing, restoration, and the recentering required to carry on the rest of your "race." Intentionally creating space in between times of busyness is a habit that supports a successful "run." Here is your first chance.

Stop and Abide

Relax

Slow down. Be present in this moment. It is the only moment you are guaranteed. God created it. Practice trust and surrender by taking five minutes to remove thoughts from yesterday and tomorrow. Turn away from your computer. Silence your phone. Step outside, regardless of the weather. Experience the air as its scent moves through your nose—God created scents. Describe the sensations of taste flowing back and forth across your tongue—God created taste. Listen to the tiniest background sounds entering your ear—God created hearing. Study the shapes, colors, forms, and lines created in the world right before your eyes—God created sight. Let your fingers roam the surfaces your hands encounter, stimulating your skin—God created touch. Learn to recharge by intentionally stopping each day to fully enjoy creation.

"I praise you because I am fearfully and wonderfully made; your works are wonderful, I know that full well" (Psalm 139:14).

Reflect

- [ ] Meditate on Psalm 23. What does this psalm reveal about your heart?

- [ ] What demands have you put on yourself that God never intended you to carry? (Matthew 11:28–30; Luke 10:40; Hebrews 3:7–11)

- [ ] What does the Bible say about rest? Does this differ from your own practice? (Exodus 16:23; Psalm 62:5; Hebrews 4:9–11)

_____

_____

_____

_____

_____

Eyes Up

Ashamed of ... *disguising, racing, scheming, neglect*

You are ... *strong, creator, shepherd, shelter*

Blessed by ... *filling, leading, protecting, comforting*

Please ... *manifest, strip, understand, stay*

Amen

2

Train

Everyone who competes in the games goes into strict training. They do it to get a crown that will not last, but we do it to get a crown that will last forever.
—1 Corinthians 9:25

What is your goal? How far are you willing to run? What pace will you aim for? How long will you train? These questions will ultimately shape your training leading up to a race. These same questions need to be asked as we run the race of life. As a Christ-follower, the Bible, Holy Spirit, and those under whom we place ourselves to be "coached" will help form our answers.

I used to run each race with the goal of beating my last time. I fervently researched the latest strategies. I read multiple reviews before purchasing new shoes. I strictly adhered to my training schedule. I limited my nutritional intake to the best fuel choices available. And what was my reward? A cheap medal that thousands of others who crossed the line also received, even if they came in dead last. I never expected to advance to a professional status. I knew I would never receive a cash reward. The race and all its excitement would end on race day. So why did I invest so much effort into running the race well?

That is a great question. Why *do* Christians pour their resources into things that offer little reward and will not last for eternity? Why do we automatically work toward accomplishing goals when, in reality, life would probably be fine without them? Might it be that Satan has his hand in distracting us from using our resources for the eternal? Absolutely! Satan encourages us to pursue the *good* in order to distract us away from God's *best*.

We will be standing before God's throne before we know it. This life is but a blink. Embracing our mortality changes how we direct our resources. If you knew you had one week to live, would you continue your rigorous training for a marathon that is a month away? Of course not! But none of us is guaranteed another day, let alone another hour of life. Satan's distractions are one reason we waste so much energy on what is not eternal. We also waste our resources because of the lie Satan fed Eve in Eden.

> The woman said to the serpent,
> "We may eat fruit from the trees in the garden, but God did say, 'You must not eat fruit from the tree that is in the middle of the garden, and you must not touch it, or you will die."
>
> *"You will not certainly die,"*
> the serpent said to the woman.
> —Genesis 3:24

Our unbelief in mortality began back in Eden. It is difficult to envision ourselves in the grave. God did not create us to taste death. It is because of disobedience that we now taste death, the phenomenon around which all Scripture centers.

For as in Adam all die, so in Christ all will be made alive.
—1 Corinthians 15:22

Another reason we waste our resources on something not guaranteed for eternity is that we do not think what we do on earth will affect eternity. We are engrossed in the moment with our desires, comforts, and pleasures. We do not consider the brevity of this life and the eternity that waits for us. Our view of the Bible, understanding of God, and heart's desires dictate where we spend our time.

For where your treasure is, there your heart will be also.
—Matthew 6:21

What is our treasure? Answering that question exposes what our hearts are working toward. If our treasure is here on earth, our hearts will work for temporary pleasure—possibly for peer approval, comfort in food, peace in vacations, or security in a savings account. If our treasure is found in heaven, our hearts will work toward blessing God's heart with what we do out of love for him. Serving people becomes a pleasure. Bringing a smile to God's face becomes our joy. Comfort, peace, and security flow from the passion we have spending in God's Word. Life on earth is a flash compared to eternity with God. Anything we have gained on earth ends the minute we cross the finish line. Anything gained for heaven's sake will be with us for all eternity.

I often sought treasure wrapped up in the here and now for the first forty years of my life. I would have been the one who would train for a marathon that was a month away when given the diagnosis of one week to live. Thankfully, this way of thinking was challenged with a season of injury, loss, and pain.

I will begin the story in January 2014, the thirty-fourth coldest winter the Midwest had seen since 1895.[1] Bursting pipes seemed to be the common plumbing trouble of the season. Snowbanks towered over cars. Our driveway was iced over with no thaw in sight. In such extreme cold, running should have been the last thing on my mind. But my fortieth birthday was days away, and I was determined to not let the phrase "over the hill" define my next decade. I was ready to begin the new year with a new commitment to staying healthy. Training for a race would be a sure way to stay motivated.

On January 2, Matt and I were tucked away in a tiny cabin in Baileys Harbor, Wisconsin. I found myself browsing a local publication titled the *Peninsula Pulse*.[2] The annual polar bear plunge, guided snowshoe hikes, and after-holiday sales filled the pages. As I closed the weekly edition of the *Pulse*, I was greeted by a full-page color ad for the annual Door County Half Marathon. On the back page was an enticing photograph of a sea of determined runners busting out of the Nicolet Bay start line, located in the pristine Peninsula State Park.[3]

The race would take place on May 3, 2014. It took seconds for me to decide that I was in. This would be a great way to begin a new decade of life. Signing up now would give me four months of training. I was ready to make this my best race ever run. Little did I know that this goal would be achieved, but in a much different way than I ever could have imagined.

Multiple injuries over the previous months had restricted my physical activity. I was ready to get moving again. I survived a rollover car accident with a couple fractured ribs in May 2013. My trusty Subaru Outback wagon lost the majority of her windows, the front axle cracked in two, and not a side of the car remained uncrushed. Walking away with a couple broken ribs was a miracle. I was left sore and sobered.

A week after this accident marked the ending of my leadership role for one of the most amazing women's small groups I had ever experienced. I was entering a year of finishing thirty graduate hours, my position at work had new expectations added, and the small group (which was actually a big group) was bursting with leadership potential. Stepping down from leading this group was a difficult decision but made the most sense at the time. Between the accident and stepping down, I was physically and emotionally bereft.

Summer vacation began a week after stepping down. Rest was pounding on my door. Summer was full. I had to complete three graduate courses and revamp my school courses. Before I knew it, it was August and time to head back to work. My mind was exhausted. I dreaded starting up a new school year. Rest would have to wait until next summer.

The beginning of this school year was followed by chronic fatigue and headaches. By the end of September, I was rushing home from work only to plop myself down on the couch for a nap. By early October, I found out that we were pregnant. This was the reason for my lack of energy. This news brought surprise and excitement. I was thirty-nine and pregnant for the first time. The planning began; we found a midwife, figured out my maternity leave, agreed on names, and began our eight-month countdown.

Matt attended an appointment with me in mid-November. We were ending the ten-week mark. It was time to listen to our baby's heartbeat. Our midwife was experienced, calm, and down-to-earth. She greeted us and then moved on quickly to the reason we were both there. She squirted the cold jelly on my beginning baby bump. She concentrated carefully as she pressed and rolled the monitor. There was nothing but static. After ten minutes of great determination, she assured us that it was still early to hear the baby's heartbeat. We left with an appointment for week twelve, hoping for better results.

The next day I started spotting. By the following evening, I sat in the emergency room, vomiting and cramping—and a bloody mess. Our baby had died. The due date was erased from the calendar. The pregnancy, planning, and excitement ended as quickly as it came. Recovery was a different story. It took months to move forward. A couple that experiences a miscarriage not only deals with the death of a life they made together, but the woman also goes through traumatic physical and hormonal changes. By the time we made it through the holidays, I was ready to move forward. The Door County Half Marathon was the thing I chose to help with just that.

Running is a natural detox for the entire body. It helps with circulation, cell regeneration, and increasing lung capacity.[4] When I run, my disc pain dissipates, energy increases, and anxiety is managed. Running is my legal drug and daily medicine. Without it, my body aches, stress rises, small issues become big, and I want to nap as soon as activities cease.

With the tragedies of the last months, my body was more than ready to get back to moving, producing those endorphins it had been deprived of and increasing my energy levels. I chose a running app,[5] entered my training goals, and created a plan. I began the plan the next day and stayed the course all the way until March 17th.

St. Patrick's Day somehow got added to our family's strong Czech cultural celebrations. Each year, we search for a restaurant with the best Irish food and entertainment. This year was no different. We ended up just down the road at our favorite family restaurant. After lots of laughs and an all-you-can-eat corned-beef-and-cabbage dinner, I headed back home.

It was late and I had a handful of chores to complete before heading to bed. Our electrician was coming the next day and I wanted to prepare the area where he would be working. I had to remove the old light fixture in the kitchen. This was an easy task. I have installed ceiling fans, chandeliers, and electrical sockets. All I had to do with this light was unscrew the fixture and then disconnect the electricity. The kitchen chair I started with did not quite lift my five-foot-three body to the height I needed to work. I kept my grandpa's antique aluminum stepladder in our hallway closet. I traded the chair for the ladder—it helped me gain a couple of inches more. I was able to take apart most of the fixture but was baffled as to why the aluminum frame remained stuck to the ceiling. I had properly disassembled the main body and removed all screws. Even after a few hard pulls, nothing happened. I figured that if I got up higher, I could create a greater torque to release the frame. I stepped onto the kitchen counter. It positioned me a bit off center from the fixture, but definitely gave me the advantage of height to help pull on the frame. I pulled. Yanked. Hung. Nothing. I retrieved a thick wooden spatula from the cooking utensil jar to use as a crowbar. Still nothing.

The clock ticked on as my frustration grew. I had to get up early for work the next morning, so I decided to give one last try. A final hang with a mighty pry and ... *bam!* A rivet from one corner of the fixture gave way. My body hurled off the counter, landing on top of the stepladder, crushing the aluminum as if it was a tin can.

Sprawled out on the floor, writhing in severe pain, I gasped for breath. The ceiling spun as time stood still. My lungs remained breathless. The pain grew. I began to pray. I was about to meet my maker. I was brought back to reality by the ringing of my phone. I moved my eyes in the direction of its ring. I remained paralyzed, without breath.

I knew it was Matt. Was this the last picture he would have of me—sprawled out on the kitchen floor beside a crushed ladder? The phone stopped ringing. I closed my eyes and tried to relax. Air began to slowly seep back into my lungs. My shallow breaths were followed by extreme stabs of pain. I ran my hand over the ribs that smashed into Grandpa's stepladder. No blood. No bones protruded from the skin. I gently rolled over to the unscathed side, lifting myself to sit. After a couple of minutes, I was able to hold on to the chair to pull myself up. I stood, staring blankly out the kitchen window into the dark of night. I was alive.

Stop and Abide

Relax

Breath—the reason we exist another moment. God fills our breath with the air he created. Focus on this involuntary process, making it voluntary. Set your timer for five minutes. Focus your stare on something pleasant. Practice equal breathing through your nose. Start breathing in for a count of four and then breathing out for a count of four. You can work yourself up to a count of six or eight. This exercise is about relaxing, not winning, so do not work up to a count that is straining. Enjoy the gift of breath.

"Then the Lord God formed a man from the dust of the ground and breathed into his nostrils the breath of life, and the man became a living being" (Genesis 2:7).

Reflect

- If you knew this was your last day on earth, what would you do differently? (Matthew 25:13; Titus 2:11–13; 1 Peter 1:23–25)

- What are treasures you can store up in heaven? (Deuteronomy 26:18; Matthew 6:19–20; Mark 10:21)

- Why do Christians neglect strict spiritual training? (Genesis 3:2–4; Luke 6:40; 1 Corinthians 9:25–27)

_____

_____

_____

_____

_____

Eyes Up

Ashamed of ... *pride, controlling, conforming, struggling*

You are ... *highest, joy, beginning, end*

Blessed by ... *mercy, pain, hope, strength*

Please ... *restore, appear, lift, heal*

Amen

3

Breath

> Let everything that has breath praise the Lord.
> —Psalm 150:6

Breath—your internal regulator. Concentration, emotions, stress level, and sleep are affected by breathing.[1] Learning to breathe properly should be one of the first functions an athlete masters. It is the next aspect of the race that we will examine.

Many idioms include breath: under one's breath, catch one's breath, in the same breath, out of breath, take away one's breath. And then there is my favorite: a breath of fresh air. Fresh air entering our lungs is a gift we often take for granted—the air that fills the edges of your nostrils with each inhale and exhale. From sucking in the wet breeze after a rainfall to the fresh scent of spring lilacs, breath gives life.

Imagine the breath you take at the end of a long day of work, the breath that is drawn in the moment you exit the workplace and hit the outdoors. This breath is slow, long, and intentional. For a second, your mind erases the stresses, to-do lists, and insults of the day. Healing takes place in this moment. And then you scurry on to the rest of the busy evening. Why do we hold out on giving ourselves this kind of breath more often? Studies suggest that relaxation and the release of anxiety may have a direct impact on our physical bodies. Anxiety, depression, heart disease, and pain are ailments that can decrease when one is regularly engaged in relaxation techniques, some of which focus on breath.[2]

> For you created my inmost being;
> you knit me together in my mother's womb.
> I praise you because
> I am fearfully and wonderfully made;
> your works are wonderful,
> I know that full well
> My frame was not hidden from you
> when I was made in the secret place,
> when I was woven together
> in the depths of the earth.
> —Psalm 139:13–15

We are fearfully and wonderfully made! The Creator made his creation with the ability to heal itself. Breathing is a function of healing. When we forget to breathe—long, slow, and deep—we turn our back on the gift God gave us. Even right now, as you are reading this, stop, close your eyes, and take three slow, deep breaths. Did you do it? How long did it take? Less than a minute? Guess how long the benefits have proven to last from such a simple exercise? Hours! We need to take time to stop throughout the day and intentionally focus on our breath.

We are given segments of time throughout life that can be considered "breath" or pause from doing something. These times are often not planned. Sometimes they create anger or anxiety. They may even be divinely appointed, encouraging us to be still. Be on the lookout for "breath." When you find it, embrace it. Fill it with anything considered life-giving. Listen to your heart and body to know what you need to embrace: journaling, reading, prayer, memorizing Scripture, time with an encouraging friend, stretching, bird watching, taking a bath, walk, or nap. Walking one minute after every mile in life demands submitting to the breath we are given.

Breath We Are Given

- traffic
- tardy clients
- delayed flights
- severance of a relationship
- injury
- extreme weather
- car trouble
- snow day
- personal limitations
- freight trains
- event cancellations

Walking one minute after every mile is not only about waiting for a breath to be given to us. It also includes creating breath. Creating breath does not happen voluntarily. We can go days, weeks, months, and even years without breath. If we hold our breath like this, we starve ourselves of life. Scheduling breath and making it a priority is vital to running the race well.

Scheduling Breath

- Block out vacations at the beginning of the year.
- Set up dates with friends at the start of the month.
- Create a plan to include daily time with the Lord.
- Schedule daily exercise.
- Begin each day by submitting to God.
- Look at your calendar each morning.
- Do not easily push aside the breath scheduled.
- Bring glory to God with your choices.
- Listen to the Holy Spirit guiding you.

Breathing is as much spiritual as it is physical. Our breath began when our Creator breathed into us. While walking in this physical world, our exhales give praise to the one who made us. On our last day granted on earth, our breath will cease, closing down our lives in this present world.

Then the LORD God formed a man from the dust of the ground and breathed into his nostrils the breath of life, and the man became a living being.
—Genesis 2:7

In his hand is the life of every creature and the breath of all mankind.
—Job 12:10

The Spirit of God has made me; the breath of the Almighty gives me life.
 —Job 33:4

When you hide your face, they are terrified; when you take away their breath, they die and return to the dust.
 —Psalm 104:29

This is what the Sovereign Lord says to these bones: I will make breath enter you, and you will come to life.
 —Ezekiel 37:5

 I knew I was alive after falling off the kitchen counter because of the return of my breath. Alive—but how well? Pain slowly filled my body as Kool-Aid fills a cup. It began on my right-side ribs, the main point of impact. The pain spread down my bicep and then into my back. I walked to the bathroom, stiff as board and slow as a snail. I gingerly removed my shirt. I examined my body in the mirror. I could only see bruises and scratches.

 Matt is an emergency-room physician's assistant. He worked in orthopedic surgery prior to his life in the emergency room. I am in good hands when it comes to medical care. Matt's calm demeanor, quick thinking, and caring heart puts him at the top of his profession. This is also true when it comes to his role as a husband. Matt is one of the most gracious, patient, and kind individuals I have ever met—that is, until I do something out of haste or compulsion.

 Matt arrived home the night of my fall after working a twelve-hour shift. He found me stripped of clothing and speechless.

When I finally shared what I had done, he examined the evidence of the crushed stepladder. No words were spoken. He came close, tenderly touched my ribs, had me take some deep breaths, and performed some movement checks. He concluded that I had probably broken some ribs, said nothing could be done, and told me to pop some pain medicine and sleep with ice.

And that was it. No pity. No helping me to bed. I was on my own with this one. I took pain reliever, tied some ice packs on, and tried to find the most comfortable position, which I came to understand did not exist. I lay awake for hours, until my exhaustion put me to sleep. Sleep would last until the slightest movement shot pain through my body. It took much effort to get out of bed—it was some sort of slide, roll, push, and whimper. The alarm clock rang too soon. I painfully got myself ready and off to work. The day challenged me in many ways. As a high school art teacher it is impossible to restrain from movement. My injury continued to swell and stiffen. By evening, fantastic color filled in the bruises, pain spread to more parts of my body, and my right arm was now out of commission.

It was six weeks before the Door County Half Marathon. Every walking step shot pain through my body. How was I going to run a race? Maybe I was not meant to run the race. I did not want to think this way. The last twelve months had been so physically limiting. I wanted to run. I began praying for a miracle.

Stop and Abide

Relax

We will continue to focus on the gift of breath. Breath is foundational to running well. It is also imperative for a multitude of other health benefits. Set your timer to five minutes. This time, try lying down on your back. Put a mat down or move to carpeting. Prop a pillow under your knees if your back is uncomfortable. Take a long, slow, deep breath through your nose. Make sure your lower belly inflates. Once your belly is full, move the air up into your chest. When topped out, take a second to pause. Then, slowly release the breath, beginning in your chest and then back down to your belly. When empty of air, take another second to pause. Then, begin the process again. Your goal is six to eight breaths per minute. Incorporate breathing exercises into daily life. When you do not have time to lie down, look for other space in your day—sitting in traffic, waiting for an appointment, feeding your baby, working at your desk, or sitting in a forever meeting. Use this time to breathe.

"The Spirit of God has made me; the breath of the Almighty gives me life" (Job 33:4).

Reflect

- ☐ How does God want you to use your breath for him? (Psalm 150:6; Acts 17:24–28; Revelation 5:12)

- ☐ Where do you need more breath in life? What can you do to create it? (Matthew 5:1; Mark 1:35; Luke 10:38–42)

- ☐ What examples in Scripture show injury resulting in sanctification? (1 Samuel 1; Acts 9:15–19; James 5:11)

_____

_____

_____

_____

_____

Jo Anna Rieger

Eyes Up

Ashamed of … *busyness, independence, greed, lust*

You are … *almighty, sustainer, redeemer, light*

Blessed by … *breath, direction, support, Jesus*

Please … *uphold, cover, cradle, still*

Amen

January. Kelly and Laura, helping celebrate my fortieth birthday in '70s style. Eight months after my car accident, two months after our miscarriage, two months before my fall, and three and a half months before the Door County Half Marathon. (Photo taken by Geri Socha)

Mid-February. Annie, standing on Lake Michigan in front of the Cana Island Lighthouse in Baileys Harbor, Wisconsin. One month before my fall and two and a half months before the Door County Half Marathon.

End of February. Demolition/remodeling in our home, which led to the changing of our kitchen light fixture, from which I fell trying to remove it. Nine weeks before the Door County Half Marathon.

March. Spring break in St. Maarten. Each morning, I would walk up to this abandoned fort and watch the sunrise from the ruins. Two weeks after my fall and four weeks before the Door County Half Marathon.

May 3, 2014. Nicolet Bay Beach, Peninsula State Park, Fish Creek, Wisconsin. Heading to the start line of the Door County Half Marathon. (Photo taken by Jane Park)

In the middle of the Door County Half Marathon. This was the 2:15 pace team I ran with.

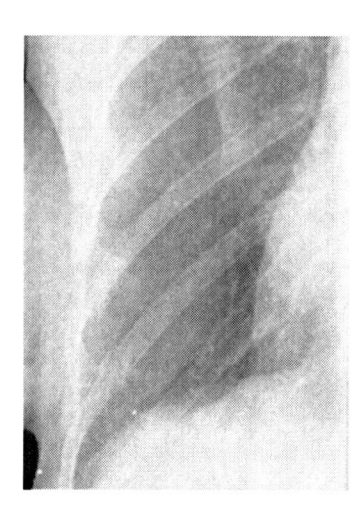

End of May. X-ray of my ribs. Nine weeks after my fall. Three weeks after the Door County Half Marathon.

June. Kangaroo Lake, Wisconsin. Matt and our niece, Hope. I spent the summer here, resting and writing. One year after my rollover car accident, seven months after our miscarriage, three months after my fall, one month after the Door County Half Marathon, and days before the death of our dear friend, Todd.

4

Heal

> Yes, my soul, find rest in God; my hope comes from him.
> —Psalm 62:5

Healing is a process that each person approaches differently. Have you considered that physical, spiritual, and emotional healing walk hand in hand? If healing encompasses all three, current treatments of the broken and sick need to change.

In the late 1990s, I was diagnosed with Methicillin-resistant Staphylococcus aureus, otherwise known as MRSA. The first known patients to be infected with MRSA were in 1961. It was only in the 1990s that MRSA began running rampant in hospitals, prisons, and nursing homes.[1] In short, it is a bacterial illness resistant to common antibiotics.

My diagnosis began with a severe sinus infection that went on for months. Antibiotics would not rid the headache, fever, and congestion. I went back to the doctor when Matt began to smell a stench coming from my nose. The doctor did an inspection of my sinus and removed an ugly, smelly, green growth. I will never forget sitting alone in the room with *it*. There *it* sat—an army green, burly growth the size of a giant lima bean. A culture was ordered. MRSA was confirmed.

I was immediately sent to the emergency room where an infectious-disease doctor met me. He placed a PICC line into the protruding vein at the bend by my left elbow. A nurse came to my home later that evening. She reviewed my medical care for the next six weeks. This should have been a wakeup call. My body was screaming for rest. At the time, I was a full-time elementary art teacher and driving into the city three times a week for nightly graduate classes. Life kept going. I carried a cooler with a portable IV pole and connected my PICC line for an antibiotic drip three times a day.

This episode was my first awakening to the connection of the body, mind, and spirit. I was sent to an immunologist upon completing the six-week IV antibiotic treatment. On my first visit, Dr. Jacobson looked me in the eye and said, "Jo Anna, you are way too young to have been this sick. You can never, ever let your body get this sick again. You need to get your physical, emotional, and spiritual world in order. Each affects the other, and one cannot be well if any of the other two are not." I thought I was going for allergy shots and came out with a lesson for life—a lesson that began my journey into true healing.

The MRSA experience was a big nudge to do life differently. One would have thought that my fall from the counter would have been the same eye-opener for my need to rest. My fall took place exactly two weeks before our school's spring break. Sue, a dear friend from grade school, had invited me to join her for a week in St. Maarten. I took her up on the offer and made flight reservations the previous summer.

It is amazing how so much can change in nine months. It was now the end of March, I was four months past a miscarriage, four weeks away from a half marathon, and recovering from a fall that severely restricted motion in my upper body. This was not the picture I had in mind when I booked my spring-break flight to paradise. Life sometimes reveals a different story than what we originally picture. How often do pictures created of the future rule our lives? How often do these pictures bring joy until they are far from becoming a reality?

Back in junior high, my mom gave me a pink sparkly plaque. This plaque sat on my bedroom dresser throughout most of my teenage life. It boldly proclaimed:

Delight yourself in the Lord, and he will give you the desires of your heart.
—Psalm 37:4

We all have dreams, visions, and desires. The Bible supports having them. I used to interpret this verse as a way to ensure that God gave me what I desired. A little praise song, a short prayer of thanksgiving, even several amens throughout the day—this was surely delighting myself in the Lord … *not!* But, if we look at Psalm 37:4 in context, we get an accurate picture of the key to dreams, visions, and desires.

> Do not fret because of those who are evil or be envious of those who do wrong; for like the grass they will soon wither, like green plants they will soon die away. Trust in the Lord and do good; dwell in the land and enjoy safe pasture. Take delight in the Lord, and he will give you the desires of your heart. Commit your way to the Lord; trust in him and he will do this: he will make your righteous reward shine like the dawn, your vindication like the noonday sun. Be still before the Lord and wait patiently for him; do not fret when people succeed in their ways, when they carry out their wicked schemes.
> —Psalm 37:1–7

In Summary

- Do not fear or be jealous.
- Trust in the Lord, and do good.
- Take delight in the Lord.
- Commit your way to the Lord.
- Be still before the Lord.
- Wait patiently for him.

In order to accomplish these, it is imperative to know who our Lord is, and pour ourselves into building a deep-rooted relationship with him. It goes way beyond listening to a Christian radio station, reading a favorite Christian blog, memorizing a verse for small group, or attending a weekend church service. I used to adhere to this recipe, until a slow and steady perseverance in God's Word and time with godly "sisters" taught me so much more.

Persevering with God is not a weekly, daily, or even hourly event. Rather, it is a minute-by-minute, second-by-second surrendering of our lives to the one who made them. A weekly church service, compulsory memorization of Scripture, and Christian radio or blogs are all good and support my walk with Christ. But, the people I see living out the first seven verses of Psalm 37 are in total surrender to God.

Surrendering to God

- Waking up in the morning with first thoughts on God
- Responding to slanderers with love and prayer
- Striving to make every moment bring glory to God
- Slowing down in the midst of chaos to lift up praise
- Recalling blessings at the end of a long, hard day

When my delight is in the Lord, my desires are aligned to his will. I can trust him, even when reality does not look like the picture I had in mind. When my picture is shattered, I am reminded that it was only of garage-sale quality when compared to the glorious masterpiece God promises. Getting to this place of acceptance is impossible on my own. Faith from God is the *only* thing that places my hope securely in something not yet seen.

Now faith is confidence in what we hope for and assurance about what we do not see.
—Hebrews 11:1

Being with Sue in St. Maarten was exactly the place to be for the season of life I was in. God's timing was perfect and his provision abundant. A journal entry during this time shows how God was working through my brokenness:

I just listened to Sidewalk Prophets sing "Make me broken so I can be healed..."[2] I laughed out loud. I'm a sore mess. *I'm learning to slow down, depend on others, and find joy in the pain.*

Sue lives with a mix of constant pain and struggle. The last year was preparing me for this trip. I was literally given a chance to walk in Sue's shoes. Because of my physical struggles I had to depend on her. Our trip included sitting for hours on the beach with the goal of healing and spending time with each other. She arranged for transportation, carried my bags, made my bed, and ensured all my needs were cared for. My half marathon training was on hold for some greater lessons.

For physical training is of some value, but godliness has value for all things, holding promise for both the present life and the life to come. That is why we labor and strive, because we have put our hope in the living God, who is the Savior of all people, and especially of those who believe.
—1 Timothy 4:8,10

Training is a disciplined regimen for an extended period of time. I never want my life in Christ to become legalistic, following a regime. But like training for an important event, our Christian life has to follow a routine. Just as the best athletes follow a prescribed training, so do those serious about following Christ.

Jesus is our example. We can start with him and then fan out to the other saints throughout Scripture. The spiritual disciplines for a follower of Christ come from studying the lives of these individuals. We find prayer, meeting together, adherence to Scripture, Sabbath, sacrifice, fasting, service, and solitude to be among the disciplines displayed throughout the Bible. This list is overwhelming and can become a legalistic checklist. When we neglect God's greatest commands of loving him and loving others, we need to question our priorities and choices, even when they are good and have to do with the church. Sometimes sanctification comes from not doing anything other than opening our hands and resting in God's care, especially when we are broken. May the busyness of accomplishing spiritual disciplines never take the place of a relationship with Jesus Christ and the church.

Stop and Abide

Relax

God made us with remarkable minds. What we put into our minds can directly affect how much control we have over the stress in our lives. Take an inventory of your day and what you let into your mind. Study this list. What can you shut off? The news? TV? Alerts on your phone? What can you allow into your mind that will bring a calm healing? Soothing music has been shown to reduce anxiety. Maybe you can open a window to listen to sounds of the outdoors. Try listening to a reading of Psalms. Or try a technology fast. Start with a couple hours, and then try an entire day. Use this time to fill your mind with anything true, pure, or lovely before God. It all comes down to guarding your ears and eyes. Take control of what you allow into your mind by shutting more off through each day and being picky with what you let in.

"Discretion will protect you, and understanding will guard you" (Proverbs 2:11).

Reflect

- What does it mean to be broken?
  (1 Samuel 2:10; Job 7:5, 17:1; Psalm 31:12)

- Describe the healing process of brokenness.
  (Proverbs 16:24; Acts 10:33; John 7:23)

- What are you being called to surrender?
  (Psalm 37:1–7; Ecclesiastes 3:1–8; Ephesians 4:22–25)

_____

_____

_____

_____

_____

Jo Anna Rieger

Eyes Up

Ashamed of ... *impatience, avoiding, anger, jealousy*

You are ... *timeless, peaceful, patient, provider*

Blessed by ... *reassuring, grace, love, fulfillment*

Please ... *protect, rejuvenate, lead, expose*

Amen

5

Pace

> What we've learned is this: God does not respond to what we do; we respond to what God does. We've finally figured it out. Our lives get in step with God and all others by letting him set the pace, not by proudly or anxiously trying to run the parade.
> —Romans 3:27–28 MSG

How many miles one runs in an hour is one's pace. Everyone's pace is different, based on physical aspects, experience, personal goals, or limitations. Setting a pace helps a runner stay within the limits of his or her body and reach goals he or she may have never thought possible.

Pace was mentioned three times in a recent sermon at church titled, "Don't Shrink God."[1] Our pastor aspires to rewire his life to a different pace. His former frantic pace was supported by the overwhelming amount of commitments on his plate. Unlike most runners who desire to ramp up their pace, our pastor shared that his new goal was to "run" a slower pace. He would accomplish this by choosing to do less with the desire of doing everything better. When we take on more than time allows we are pushed into a faster pace to try and get everything in. This adds stress to everything we do, effects our emotions, strips us of time for restoration, and decreases the quality of our output.

I try to find the "nugget" in every sermon. The "nugget" is something I learned that I want to take away and apply to my life. The "nugget" of this sermon was: *even if I could do a lot more, I should not.* This was the first time I had heard this statement from the pulpit. I spent a lifetime in church being told:

- You have all eternity to rest.
- Work out your salvation with fear and trembling.
- Everything you do should be unto the glory of God.

I strived to live out each one of these statements. My hard work was praised. I feared idleness, as I believed it was sin. I neglected physical and emotional pain, feeling a stronger obligation to build God's kingdom for eternity. I memorized Proverbs 31 in multiple translations and tried to be this woman:

> A good woman is hard to find, and worth far more than diamonds. Her husband trusts her without reserve, and never has reason to regret it. Never spiteful, she treats him generously all her life long. She shops around for the best yarns and cottons, and enjoys knitting and sewing. She's like a trading ship that sails to faraway places and brings back exotic surprises. She's up before dawn, preparing breakfast for her family and organizing her day. She looks over a field and buys it, then,

with money she's put aside, plants a garden. First thing in the morning, she dresses for work, rolls up her sleeves, eager to get started. She senses the worth of her work, is in no hurry to call it quits for the day. She's skilled in the crafts of home and hearth, diligent in homemaking. She's quick to assist anyone in need, reaches out to help the poor. She doesn't worry about her family when it snows; their winter clothes are all mended and ready to wear. She makes her own clothing, and dresses in colorful linens and silks. Her husband is greatly respected when he deliberates with the city fathers. She designs gowns and sells them, brings the sweaters she knits to the dress shops. Her clothes are well-made and elegant, and she always faces tomorrow with a smile. When she speaks she has something worthwhile to say, and she always says it kindly. She keeps an eye on everyone in her household, and keeps them all busy and productive. Her children respect and bless her; her husband joins in with words of praise: Many women have done wonderful things, but you've outclassed them all! Charm can mislead and beauty soon fades. The woman to be admired and praised is the woman who lives in the Fear-of-God. Give her everything she deserves! Festoon her life with praises!
—Proverbs 31:10–31 MSG

Where did this leave me? Running life at an extreme pace over an extended period. I became an ultra-marathon Christian. I was so busy doing good that I could never enjoy God. My heart was left broken and damaged. I was numb to my own needs, which carried over to others as well. I honored God by what I thought he wanted me to do. I followed rules I thought honored God, but living a life like this was anything but honoring to God. Busyness distracted me from God's best.

These people honor me with their lips, but their hearts are far from me. They worship me in vain; their teachings are merely human rules.
—Matthew 15:8–9

He has shown you, O mortal, what is good. And what does the LORD require of you? To act justly and to love mercy and to walk humbly with your God.
—Micah 6:8

Do you not know that your bodies are temples of the Holy Spirit, who is in you, whom you have received from God? You are not your own; you were bought at a price. Therefore honor God with your bodies.
—1 Corinthians 6:19–20

This pace was not something that crept up on me. This pace was rooted deep in systems from my youth. By age five, I knew what hell was and did not want to go there. I knelt by my bed one night with Mom and asked Jesus to forgive all the bad I had done. I told him I believed what the Bible said about him. The problem was that my walk with Christ was all in my head and had not reached my heart. I became a slave to service for God. Busyness in the physical church building among the people who attended it had become my god.

The condition of my heart was clearly exposed back in December of 2000. It was so damaged by the pace and rules I had so carefully followed. My priorities were set on pursuits that would not make a difference even five years down the road. It was a cold winter evening when I received a call at church. It was the sixth night in a row that I was busy working on the lady's Christmas tea. My grandmother had struggled with cancer for the last couple of years. Due to everything on my plate, I left going to see my grandma for the weekend after the tea, when I would finally have time to visit.

Cell phones were not yet in the pockets of most people; thus, the call that night came to the church office. I left my wreath-decorating post and went to answer the call. It was my mom. She solemnly stated that Grandma was not doing well. I left everything and sped over to my parents' home, where Grandma was living. I arrived to see two squad cars in the driveway. I ran inside to find everyone crying around a lifeless body. I was too late. Grandma was dead. My world was rocked. I was grieving God in my misunderstood view of what I thought would please him. My heart had some serious issues that I needed to deal with.

> I have looked at myself in the mirror every morning and asked myself, "If today were the last day of my life, would I want to do what I am about to do today?" And whenever the answer is "no" for too many days in a row, I know I need to change something.
> —Steve Jobs[2]

Change can be scary as it ventures into the unknown. However, when the known is not bringing about anything good, it is the perfect time to reevaluate life. I love Steve Jobs's quote about needing to change, but it needs one addition: "If today were the last day of my life, would God want me to do what I am about to do today?" Joy comes when our lives are in line with what God deems important. What we spend time on would also change if we believed each breath was a gift that could end in a second.

A major drive for change is understanding who God is. Actually, we can never fully understand who God is. He is so much more than our tiny brains can grasp. But God has graciously made multiple ways to get to know him: the Bible, creation, and his Son, Jesus Christ. When we begin a study of all three, we are bombarded with knowledge of who the God of the universe is. Below are attributes that can be found when studying to understand who God is.

God

- has everything under control.
- is 100 percent trustworthy.
- desires a relationship with me.
- is love.
- knows everything.
- wants the best for me.
- is eternal.

Anxiety is squashed whenever I meditate on these attributes. *Meditating* is the crucial word. In order to meditate, I have to stop and slow down. It is only when I have made a change in pace that I can even begin to consider who God is and what Scripture has to offer my situation. Slowing down allows me to get my eyes off circumstances and on God. This is where the answers are. Stopping enables me to step out in faith, believing God for what he promises.

Shortly after signing up for the Door County Marathon in January and prior to my fall in March, my friend from California flew in for a visit. I had met Annie a couple of years earlier when she lived in the Chicagoland area. She attended my church. Annie requested to be placed in a small group near home. I was the small-group leader with the closest group to Annie's home. All it took was one phone call and Annie joined our group the following week. Annie *happened* to pull my name out of a hat, and I became her accountability partner for the months to follow. The rest is history.

Annie missed her winters, so our trip included heading north. We had a delightful weekend in Door County, Wisconsin—sledding, a candlelit night hike, walking the frozen shore of Lake Michigan, warming by the fire, and plenty of hot tea. The weather report forecasted a snowstorm for the morning of our departure. I disregarded this warning, as snowstorms seemed to be the norm that winter. My Subaru Outback could handle most weather; thus, I took Annie to the Door County Bakery[3] for fresh-baked cinnamon rolls and coffee. We savored every last lick of frosting, packed up, and began making our way back down to Illinois.

Wind gusts picked up at the beginning of our southern descent. Snow lightly scattered across the road. The flurries increased. The wind took every flake, throwing it relentlessly at the road. Visibility was limited. Conditions worsened the longer we drove. The snow stirred and whipped on the highway in front of us. The car swayed. The tires began to fail the road. All traffic disregarded the sixty-five miles per hour signs and we crawled at a mere twenty-five miles per hour.

I had to teach the next day and Annie had a flight first thing in the morning. If I was alone, I probably would have given up for the day. Annie put on soft music, asked lots of fun questions, and made sure I was comfortable. When she saw I needed a break, she would find some excuse to get me to exit the highway.

I will never forget our conversation. Annie is a small-aircraft pilot. She has had the experience of flying in all kinds of weather. Annie understood the conditions in which I was driving; thus, she carefully steered our conversation. "Whenever flying, you have to focus. Regardless of anything else happening around you—failing instruments, poor weather, lack of communication—you have to focus on your mission of flying the plane and landing it safely. Put out of your mind anything that is making the flight other than perfect. Focus. Focus brings the peace needed to fly in a storm."

And I focused. My knuckles relaxed. I began to breathe. What normally takes four hours to drive took us seven hours. The pace was not quite what I was used to or had planned on. However, if I had kept the pace of sixty-five miles per hour, we would have ended up in a ditch like the five other cars we passed on our way. I completed the mission. We arrived home safely because I chose an appropriate pace and a friend helped me focus.

The words "once more" indicate the removing of what can be shaken—that is, created things—so that what cannot be shaken may remain.
—Hebrews 12:27

A runner constantly considers his or her pace. The beginning pace will differ from the last thirty seconds of the race. Adjustments are needed if the air temperature is burning hot or bitterly cold. Elevations and declines will obviously affect the pace as well. Age, training, and physical wellness all play a part in the runner's pace.

Our pace in life's race must be based on the circumstances that surround us. We should not force ourselves to go beyond what we can accomplish with health and safety. Each season's pace must be carefully considered. Some seasons will allow us to take on much. Other times, we will encounter hardships that require us to slow down, considering what essentials are needed to continue the race. The essentials come down to our purpose on earth and our future in eternity. If we focus on the eternal and let the Holy Spirit set our pace, we can handle almost any road, along with the conditions that surround us.

Stop and Abide

Relax

God created us with miraculous minds and bodies that have the potential to heal. Movement relaxes the body. In the middle of your day, stop what you are doing. Take a few minutes to move—walk around the block, walk up and down several flights of stairs, do some head rolls or shoulder shrugs. When you return to whatever you were doing, notice the increase in attention you have gained by taking a break to move. In order to focus on your goal, you need to take a break and move.

"For you created my inmost being; you knit me together in my mother's womb. I praise you because I am fearfully and wonderfully made; your works are wonderful, I know that full well" (Psalm 139:13–14).

Reflect

- How would you describe a godly pace?
  (Genesis 2:2; Numbers 14:18; 2 Peter 3:8)

- How do you honor God with your body?
  (Proverbs 14:31; Romans 12:1–2; 1 Corinthians 6:19–20)

- What needs to be removed from your life to sharpen your focus on the eternal? (Isaiah 30:7–8; 1 Thessalonians 5:1–11; Hebrews 12:27)

_____

_____

_____

_____

_____

Jo Anna Rieger

Eyes Up

Ashamed of ... *lying, losing, indifference, defeat*

You are ... *generous, fair, ultimate, truth*

Blessed by ... *difficulties, friends, vision, presence*

Please ... *defend, renew, reset, saturate*

Amen

6

Gear

> For our struggle is not against flesh and blood, but against the rulers, against the authorities, against the powers of this dark world, and against the spiritual forces of evil in the heavenly realms. Therefore put on the full armor of God, so that when the day of evil comes, you may be able to stand your ground, and after you have done everything, to stand.
> —Ephesians 6:12–13

The successful runner thoughtfully considers his or her gear. Footwear, clothing, hydration, and fuel are part of these considerations. Having the right gear can make or break the race. We struggle when not properly geared up. This is also true of our race in life.

Ephesians 6:12–13 touches on our "real" struggle. We often center on events or conditions that are visible, sure that this is where our struggle lies. However, the real struggle is against the spiritual forces of evil, working against our good. These spiritual forces often aim for the mind, with the goal of obscuring truth.

When our minds are not guided by truth, we follow a lie. Satan feeds us lies that halt our race to an abrupt stop:

- This is never going to end.
- You can't do this.
- It's going to hurt.
- You aren't good enough.
- You'll never change.
- No one will understand.
- You'll never make it.

Focusing on these lies distracts us from God's truth. When distracted from God's truth, we often concentrate on conditions that create a not-so-perfect reality. Our anxiety goes through the roof, and our peace is stolen. This distracted focus makes it impossible to think like Christ.

In chapter five, I shared about my drive through a monster of a snowstorm. I found peace in the midst of a storm because a friend redirected my mind. Annie shared truth that could not immediately be seen in the storm. She moved my focus off the conditions that surrounded us. She told fun stories. She selected songs of worship that fed our hearts and minds. She centered our conversation on how God was at work. One of the ugliest drives turned into a life lesson and fond memory.

God designed us with the need to focus on him. A focus on who God is and what he promises has the power to change the reality we experience, bringing peace where chaos would otherwise abound. We have the power to bring anxiety or peace into our lives by what we choose to focus our minds on.

Those with sound thoughts you will keep in peace, in peace because they trust in you.
—Isaiah 26:3 CEB

One of my first gear checks before heading out on a long run is making sure I have something to focus my mind on. You may not be going out for a long run but instead may be heading out for another mundane day at work, beginning a demanding day at home with the kids, or starting a long, lonely weekend alone. Everyone is at a different place in life's race. Regardless of what route we are on as Christians, we need to thoughtfully plan out our gear. Our gear suits us up for life's struggles, leaving no margin for a battle of the mind. The rest of this chapter will concentrate on the three disciplines I use to gear up my mind: God's Word, prayer, and worship.

And do not set your heart on what you will eat or drink; do not worry about it. For the pagan world runs after all such things, and your Father knows that you need them. But seek his kingdom, and these things will be given to you as well.
—Luke 12:29–31

God's Word

We must focus on what is true and life-giving. God's Word is defined as such. This is the first piece of gear that is essential for running the race well. Scripture fights our struggles. We must meditate on Scripture daily and hide it in our hearts. If we are disciplined to gear up our minds with Scripture, we will be ready for any inclement circumstances that enter our lives. We will end each day focused and strong, based on where we set our minds. The following passage is one of my favorites in this endeavor:

> Rejoice in the Lord always. I will say it again: Rejoice! ... Do not be anxious about anything, but in every situation, by prayer and petition, with thanksgiving, present your requests to God. And the peace of God, which transcends all understanding, will guard your hearts and your minds in Christ Jesus. Finally, brothers and sisters, whatever is true, whatever is noble, whatever is right, whatever is pure, whatever is lovely, whatever is admirable—if anything is excellent or praiseworthy—think about such things.
> —Philippians 4:4, 6–8

Memorizing Scripture takes time and hard work, but then, anything of worth requires this. The worth of memorizing Scripture is that it becomes one with your spirit. It comes to your mind throughout the day. Certain passages resurrect themselves when specific needs come along. Memorized Scripture also naturally exits your mouth when praying. Philippians 4:6 is one of those verses for me.

Everyone needs to come up with his or her own plan for memorizing Scripture. Prior to technology, I used a note card to help memorize Scripture. This note card went everywhere I did. By the time I actually mastered the verse, that note card would be soggy, bent, and smeared. It did its job, though. I ran long distances, staying focused and strong. I now have hundreds of verses that I can pull up from memory for just about any circumstance.

Technology has improved my method of memorization. I now use digital flash cards[1] and a Bible memory game.[2] Both are apps for my phone. The digital flash cards post the verse's reference on one side and the actual verse on the other. The flash cards can be organized into different categories. My mastery of each card can also be rated, helping me spend time on memorizing where needed.

The Bible memory game app allows me to choose which verse(s) I want to memorize and how many words I want hidden. I then have to guess the missing words. It is like the old chalkboard game we would play in Sunday school, where the teacher would have us erase one word at a time from the verse we were learning until we knew the whole passage by memory.

Anxiety is a battle of the heart and mind. It is often birthed out of faulty desires and logic. The Bible is so much more than a bunch of pages with words. The words of Scripture are power. They are truth. They are life. They break the chains of anxiety, fear, and depression. They tune our hearts to God's heart. Anxiety robs us of God's promises. Sandwiched between fear and depression, anxiety fogs the mind from the plan God has for us. The majority of our anxiety has absolutely nothing to do with the reality we are in. It has everything to do with the fears we project about the past, present, or future.

I used to think anxiety was a condition I inherited from my family. It was not until I surrendered my life to the authority of Jesus Christ that I tasted victory over anxiety's control. When I rely on God, surrender to his timing, live in his presence, acknowledge his perfect ways, and bring my mind to praise, anxiety fails to exist. Memorizing God's Word helps me do this.

Your word is a lamp for my feet, a light on my path.
    —Psalm 119:105

For no word from God will ever fail.
    —Luke 1:37

Sanctify them by the truth; your word is truth.
    —John 17:17

For the word of God is alive and active. Sharper than any double-edged sword …
    —Hebrews 4:12

Prayer

Daniel was recorded as getting on his knees three times a day to pray. The disciples went to the temple mound during the hours of prayer. First Thessalonians 5:17 instructs us to pray continuously. Jesus most likely followed the Jewish custom of praying in the morning, afternoon, and evening. Prayer is definitely optimal gear for a successful run in life. Prayer immediately rips our hearts and minds off of what lies before us, focusing them on God.

Prayer is entering the throne room of the God of this universe. He holds your every breath in his almighty hands. Try aligning your body in a position that redirects your mind to what you are doing. Bow your head. Kneel. Lie on the ground. Try praying with your palms lifted up, a position of surrender and submission. Release control of life into your maker's care.

There are many prayers throughout the Bible that align to exactly what we are experiencing today. Our prayers can follow these examples. These scriptural prayers show that kneeling before God is not about giving him our list of wants. Scriptural prayers demonstrate confession of sins, proclamation of the attributes of God, thanksgiving, and presentation of needs, according to God's will. One of the greatest examples of prayer comes straight from Jesus:

> Our Father in heaven, hallowed be your name, your kingdom come, your will be done, on earth as it is in heaven. Give us today our daily bread. And forgive us our debts, as we also have forgiven our debtors. And lead us not into temptation, but deliver us from the evil one.
> —Matthew 6:9–13

We have to be careful to never blindly follow rules set up by man. God is interested in our hearts. In fact, the Lord's

Prayer—the title commonly given to Matthew 6:9–13—was written as a response to how the religious leaders prayed. Jesus condemned their empty prayers prayed in public and wanted to demonstrate prayer from a heart that understands who God is.

The acronym CATS (some people use the order ACTS) taught me how to pray scriptural prayers. C stands for confession, A stands for adoration, T stands for thanksgiving, and S stands for supplication. Not all prayers will include each letter of CATS, but it is a good foundation on which to build a prayer. Prayer goes way beyond asking God for our desires. Prayer is communication with the almighty creator of the universe and should put us quickly on our knees. Using CATS can help bring understanding to the seriousness of prayer and how to communicate with God. The "Eyes Up" section at the end of each chapter in this book is actually a poetic prayer that follows this acronym. The Bible is full of prayers that demonstrate parts of CATS.

Confession:

Then I acknowledged my sin to you and did not cover up my iniquity. I said, "I will confess my transgressions to the Lord." And you forgave the guilt of my sin.
    —Psalm 32:5

I said, "Have mercy on me, Lord; heal me, for I have sinned against you."
    —Psalm 41:4

Wash away all my iniquity and cleanse me from my sin.
—Psalm 51:2

Adoration:

There is no one holy like the LORD; there is no one besides you; there is no Rock like our God.
—1 Samuel 2:2

God, the blessed and only Ruler, the King of kings and Lord of lords, who alone is immortal and who lives in unapproachable light, whom no one has seen or can see. To him be honor and might forever. Amen.
—1 Timothy 6:15–16

Day and night they never stop saying: "Holy, holy, holy is the Lord God Almighty, who was, and is, and is to come."
—Revelation 4:8

Thanksgiving:

Give thanks to the LORD, for he is good; his love endures forever.
—1 Chronicles 16:34

The LORD is my strength and my shield; my heart trusts in him, and he helps me. My heart leaps for joy, and with my song I praise him.
—Psalm 28:7

Therefore, since we are receiving a kingdom that cannot be shaken, let us be thankful, and so worship God acceptably with reverence and awe.
—Hebrews 12:28

Supplication:

But as for me, I am poor and needy; come quickly to me, O God. You are my help and my deliverer; Lord, do not delay.
 —Psalm 70:5

As Jesus went on from there, two blind men followed him, calling out, "Have mercy on us, Son of David!"
 —Matthew 9:27

He went away a second time and prayed, "My Father, if it is not possible for this cup to be taken away unless I drink it, may your will be done."
 —Matthew 26:42

In addition to praying CATS, one might consider using a "daily office,"[3] another tool to support regular prayer throughout the day. The daily office is a spiritual discipline focusing on praying Scripture and hymns throughout the day. The daily office has been around for centuries and may also be referred to as the divine hours, liturgy of the hours, common lectionary,[4] and common prayer.[5] Some daily offices are organized into eight sessions a day. Some contemporary versions are divided into three daily sessions. How many times have we started the day in prayer, focusing on God, only to drag through the rest of the day without another thought of Jesus or his Word? The daily office can be used as a tool to intentionalize our walks with God, setting up appointed stops for refocus and renewal. We are told to pray without ceasing. The daily office assists in being consistent with praying throughout the entire day.

Having a prayer journal is another tool an individual may use to build the habit of prayer. Journaling brings us into a safe environment. It creates a place to have a conversation with God. The words poured out on the pages can be revisited in time. Growth, digression, highs, and lows are all recorded and learned from. A prayer journal adds a physical presence to the spiritual discipline of prayer. I use a journal app[6] on my phone. In fact, most of this book was written by tap-typing, using this journal. I support electronic journals because they allow reflection during any part of the day. Scripture can easily be copied and pasted to an electronic journal. The journal can be printed and bound into a book at the end of the year. A search engine makes looking up anything recorded in an electronic journal a snap.

Regardless of one's method for prayer, it comes down to carving out time to kneel before God's throne. What can you do to make sure you are not neglecting this key spiritual discipline? I have a morning, noon, and evening reminder that comes up on my phone that says, "Pray." When we release control back into the hands of the one who had it all in the first place, life looks much different. Prayer is a time to filter everything that has happened in the day through God's eyes. It is a way to refocus our minds, making sure we are on the right path.

More than anything you guard, protect your mind, for life flows from it. ... Focus your eyes straight ahead; keep your gaze on what is in front of you. Watch your feet on the way, and all your paths will be secure.
    —Proverbs 4:23, 25–6 CEB

Worship

Psalm 119 speaks of King David praising God seven times a day. Worship is the third piece of gear that will ensure a successful run in life. Worship is the reverent act or bringing to God all the glory that is due to him. It is giving God his proper worth and making ourselves low. Worship can involve speaking, listening, or doing. Worship is the *A* in CATS.

Music can easily lend itself to worship, but do not be fooled. Just because a song is played on a Christian radio station or has been printed in a hymnal for the last one hundred years does *not* mean it is worship. Worshipful music has to lift our eyes *up*. I am not referring to music with harps or lyrics that mention the sky. Worship has nothing to do with instrumental or stylistic preferences. Worship *does* require unity within the body and tapping into the same power released by Scripture. Lyrics *must* remind us that God is big and challenge the way we view circumstances and self. We are called to worship God in spirit and truth (John 4:24). Music must pass this test in order to be called worship. Otherwise, it is just another noise in the universe. Once we taste true worship, our hearts and minds will long for nothing less.

I am fussy about my running playlists. It is sometimes the only space I have in a day to bring my health to a better place. I take time each month to download new worship music and program playlists that ensure healing. Each race I run has a special playlist created with every mile in mind. Jon Guerra's "I Will Follow" made it to my 2014 Door County Half Marathon playlist. It was the perfect choice and pumped me up the two times it played during the race. It focuses on who I will follow and how it can look when ending life's race. I have included the lyrics to help you taste worshipful music that will inspire "running" well:

I Will Follow

When the sea is calm and all is right
When I feel Your favor flood my life
Even in the good, I'll follow You
Even in the good, I'll follow You

When the boat is tossed upon the waves
When I wonder if You'll keep me safe
Even in the storms, I'll follow You
Even in the storms, I'll follow You

I believe everything that You say You are
I believe that I have seen Your unchanging heart
In the good things and in the hardest part
I believe and I will follow You
I believe and I will follow You

When I see the wicked prospering
When I feel I have no voice to sing
Even in the want, I'll follow You
Even in the want, I'll follow You

When I find myself so far from home
And You lead me somewhere I don't wanna go
Even in my death, I'll follow You
Even in my death, I'll follow You

When I come to end this race I've run
And I receive the prize that Christ has won
I will be with You in Paradise
I will be with You in Paradise

Stop and Abide

Relax

Our bodies are the temple of the Holy Spirit. What we put into our body is actually an act of worship. Food that benefits our health also brings God glory. Caffeine, sugar, and processed foods are all foods that exacerbate or induce anxiety. To help your mental well-being try changing your diet. Make at least one healthy change for today, and then gradually make more changes with each new day, week, or month. Try water or herbal tea instead of coffee or soda pop. Use vegetables, nuts, or dried fruit instead of candy and chips. Drink a fresh fruit, frozen smoothie instead of ice cream.

"Don't you know that you yourselves are God's temple and that God's Spirit dwells in your midst?" (1 Corinthians 3:16)

Reflect

- What should your mind be focused on throughout the day? (Matthew 5:16; Luke 9:23–25; Hebrews 13:16)

- What "gear" do you need to help you in life's race? (Ephesians 6:10–18)

- What is the condition of a healthy "heart"? (Matthew 5:8; Matthew 6:21; Mark 12:30; Luke 12:29)

_____

_____

_____

_____

_____

_____

Jo Anna Rieger

Eyes Up

Ashamed of … *independence, wavering, prying, apathy*

You are … *salvation, sustenance, compassion, grace*

Blessed by … *seasons, song, new life, promises*

Please … *reveal, regenerate, radiate, return*

Amen

7

Race

> He gives strength to the weary and increases the power of the weak. Even youths grow tired and weary, and young men stumble and fall; but those who hope in the Lord will renew their strength. They will soar on wings like eagles; they will run and not grow weary, they will walk and not be faint.
> —Isaiah 40:29–31

It was May. The annual Door County Half Marathon had finally arrived. This race differed from others in that I was not alone; I was running with a friend. Back in January, I sent out an email invite for a couple others to join me in the race. To my surprise, Jane responded.

Jane is one of the busiest people I know. She never advertises her busyness or makes you feel like you are invading on her precious time. Rather, she is all ears in your presence. Her voice replies with slow, thoughtful questions that bring any conversation to an honest place. It was an honor to have her join me and definitely God's plan from the beginning. This book would never have been written without Jane being a piece of the puzzle.

We began our pre-race preparations on Friday, after a long hard week of work. These preparations started with a four hour drive up to Door County, Wisconsin. The stress of the week melted away the moment we stepped foot into the car. This is the gift of a friend who brings peace to your world. Jane loves Jesus. This is the peace she brings to my world. Peace comes when hearts are focused on the eternal. Life will always be full of stress. If your life is not, just call some of your friends or turn on the news, and it will be. To run the race of life well, we need friends who help take our gaze off what is happening around us and move our eyes up to God. He has it all under control, loves us tremendously, and wants to give us the best.

I awoke Saturday morning before the first sign of daybreak. The race was still hours away, but my checklist was already slowly being completed:

> iTunes playlist--check
> Gear--check
> Nutrition--check
> Hydration--check
> Map the course--check
> Parking instructions--check
> Relaxation techniques--check
> Warm-ups
> Stretches
> Porta Potty stop

I like to leave plenty of margin on race day. It creates a calm in the midst of what can be a chaotic event. We arrived at Peninsula State Park with time to spare. After scoping out the post-race party tents, we strolled over to the crowded start line.

Jane is not only a sister in Christ but also a gifted physical therapist who understands the body and its balances. Knowing our capabilities, Jane had chosen a pace for the race. The pace she chose was thirty-three minutes slower than my last half marathon. I would have never considered such a pace prior to my fall. At this point, six weeks after a traumatic injury, I was lucky to even be entering the race. My goal was to cross the line. I had no idea if I would be able to keep up with Jane's pace. I knew the encouragement of a friend would be vital, so I wanted to try to stick with her if at all possible.

We looked for our pace team of 2:15 (a finish time of two hours and fifteen minutes). Each pacer holds a flag by which to identify him or her. The Door County Half Marathon's pace teams consisted of eight groups:

    1:45
    1:50
    1:55
    2:00
    2:05
    2:10
    2:15
    2:25

The faster paces were positioned closest to the start line. Our team was toward the back of the crowd, as it was the second-to-last group. Upon finding our group, we noticed two flags held in our pace team. This meant there were two pacers. Jane gravitated toward the older gentleman with defined muscles, bleached-blond hair, a goatee, and ponytail. The only equipment on his body, besides a pace flag, was a metal analog watch.

Minutes before the race began, this pacer gathered his team of runners close around. He introduced himself as Tim, a native of Appleton, Wisconsin. He described the strategy he was going to use for the race. We would walk at each mile marker for a total of one minute. When the minute was up we would crank up the pace to make up for the time spent walking. We also would walk up all hills. Tim said he would let us go at the last mile, encouraging us to run our hardest. He guaranteed we would pass most runners along the way, finishing strong.

Tim's strategy sounded un-race-like. I did not know if I wanted to be a part of a large group of walkers, disrupting the flow of other runners. I wanted to join the group gathered around the other 2:15 pacer, who was taking his team straight to the finish without walking. I figured Jane felt the same way.

I figured wrong. Jane turned to me, smiling with relief. She was thrilled we had found Tim and was looking forward to his strategy. Jane had read about this running technique, which was actually developed by Jeff Galloway, a former Olympian and world-renowned trainer.[1]

I was committed to run with Jane. I submitted to the fact that I was going to do some walking this race and might annoy other runners. We aligned ourselves behind Tim, I let go of my picture of what this race was to look like, and we were off.

The race began as a slow crawl. The multitude of participants eagerly approached the start line. Spectators cheered from the sidelines while ringing cowbells. The first few minutes were tight, leaving very little room between runners. Tim was easy to spot with his flag and white ponytail. Jane and I stayed close, running side by side. We were in a groove, feeling good, when Tim yelled, "Walk!"

We completed the first mile. Volunteers frantically passed out water to the sea of runners rushing by. In past races, I would run with a sleek water bottle. I did not want to lose a second in the muddled mass of racers trying to quench their thirst at water stations. I took the below verse more serious in my earthly race than my spiritual race.

Do you not know that in a race all the runners run, but only one gets the prize? Run in such a way as to get the prize.
—1 Corinthians 9:24

However, this race was different. I did not bring anything extra for this race. No watch, heart-rate monitor, or water bottle. Stripping myself of all extra components had been freeing. On the other hand, walking a minute after the first mile was humbling. I had not even built up a sweat. There I walked, feeling the breeze of the other runners whiz by. I was stuck walking another thirty seconds.

At the end of our first minute, Tim yelled, "Running!" Our pack of followers quickly joined his pace, and we continued on. Because our pace involved a one-minute walk after every mile, we picked up our pace each time we restarted. We would eventually pass the other 2:15 team that did not walk during the race, only for them to pass us at the next mile marker when our minute of walking began. The race pretty much continued this same way. We would run, and just about the time we started to feel the effects of the race, it was the end of a mile—time to walk and hydrate. The more miles we ran, the easier walking became. Although this strategy seemed counterintuitive to being in a race, it was fun to be doing something the majority of the others runners would never dare try.

Jane and I enjoyed a light conversation as we trusted our pace to Tim. The walking and water rejuvenated us each mile. Others runners in our pace team had a profound impact on our race experience as well. We were grouped with some of the best cheerleaders around. They would randomly break out in songs and chants, leaving our team with smiles. My mind focused on anything but split times or passing other runners. Pain was absent. My old definition of running a race was being redefined. God opened my eyes to a more abundant way of doing life. Because of injury, I was willing to surrender. I ran in a way that I never would have allowed myself to run before being injured.

Injury and submission also brought me to a healthier and happier way of running life's race. I love that Scripture uses the race as a metaphor for how we need to do life. How would our days look if each morning we fixed our eyes on a pacer? What if we did life with a pace team that all had their hearts set on the same goal? How would life look if we had a friend who encouraged and ran alongside us the entire race?

The Church is our pace team. When I use the word Church, I am not talking about a building, but the people surrendered to Jesus Christ as Lord and Savior.

On top of joining a "pace team," we will benefit from picking one person to partner up with in life. This person should never be afraid to ask the hard questions and should be in our faces on a daily basis, making sure we are becoming more like Christ.

We all need a pacer. For the Christian, Jesus is our pacer. We need to fix our eyes on him in every step taken in this life. We can trust him. He has all the strategies worked out. We can leave all our extras behind, knowing he will provide. We just need to get 100 percent in line with his steps. He will always be right in front of us if we choose to run with him.

Jesus is also committed to never leaving us. This was unlike Tim, who needed a bathroom break in the middle of the race. This actually threw off our team for a couple of miles. Those couple of miles were unsettling. We kept looking for Tim and could not find him. We did not know if our pace was accurate. Our group began to scatter, and the powerful team effort was slowly fading. Guess who ended up passing us after a couple of miles of running on our own? Tim! By this time, Jane and I had lost the entire team, and we were on our own. We quickly got behind our leader and were thrilled to have him bring us home to the finish line.

Jesus is always there. The only time he is out of sight is when our eyes fall down on the road or wander to the sidelines. Everything gets off track when this happens. It is amazing how quickly life snaps back in order when we finally look up and follow our Leader.

I lift up my eyes to you, to you who sit enthroned in heaven.
 —Psalm 123:1

Never will I leave you; never will I forsake you.
 —Hebrews 13:5

Mile twelve. We made it! We were still talking to each other, no injuries, and ready to take on the last mile to the finish line. At the beginning of the race, Tim had explained that at the last mile he would cheer us on to go all out. He promised we would pass other runners, as we would have run in a way that allowed our bodies to heal between each mile. Upon crossing the mile twelve marker, Jane and I left each other with a "See you at the finish line!"

I slowly pulled ahead of the other runners. I did not feel pain, so I decided to fire it up. My little legs cranked away, carrying me past everyone I came upon. A mile is a drop in the bucket compared to the twelve I had already completed. I was not worried about burning out. I would have all the rest in the world in minutes. I focused on finishing well and was able to do so because of the method Tim used.

Before I knew it, a loud speaker announced, "Jo Anna Rieger from Lombard, Illinois." I was now steps away from the finish line. The sound of my name, along with the crowds cheering, pushed my pace even faster. And then … I crossed the line. The race was over. I finished strong. I was handed a medal, a banana, and a cup of water. Little did I know this ending was, in fact, the beginning of a new way of doing life.

Stop and Abide

Relax

What your mind focuses on impacts the level of anxiety you experience. Decide right now to clear your mind of any negative or stressful feelings. Do not let them back in. Satan so wants to bring you down by keeping your focus on what you have no control over. Scripture reminds us to think about whatever is lovely, pure, and true. Do just this: close your eyes and focus on pleasant images from the past or possibilities of the future. Maybe you are in an environment in which you can keep your eyes open to focus on the beauty around you. With what has God blessed you? What does he promise? Take your thoughts captive, placing them on God, and peace will follow.

"Finally, brothers and sisters, whatever is true, whatever is noble, whatever is right, whatever is pure, whatever is lovely, whatever is admirable—if anything is excellent or praiseworthy—think about such things. Whatever you have learned or received or heard from me, or seen in me—put it into practice. And the God of peace will be with you" (Philippians 4:8–9).

Reflect

- When is it appropriate to walk in the race of life? (Matthew 11:28–29; Luke 23:55–56)

- When is it appropriate to run with everything you have? (1 Corinthians 9:24; Romans 16:12; Colossians 4:12–13)

- How does hoping in the Lord renew strength? (Psalm 130:7; Isaiah 40:29–31)

_____

_____

_____

_____

_____

Jo Anna Rieger

Eyes Up

Ashamed of … *fearing, impressing, perfecting, wasting*

You are … *calling, seeing, saving, forgiving*

Blessed by … *provisions, compassion, wisdom, peace*

Please … *assure, guide, calm, unveil*

Amen

8

Recover

> The Lord is my shepherd, I lack nothing.
> He makes me lie down in green pastures,
> he leads me beside quiet waters,
> he refreshes my soul.
> He guides me along the right paths
> for his name's sake.
> —Psalm 23:1–3

Painful experiences filled most of the last twelve months. Reflecting on pain can inspire change. Pain sometimes signifies a need for healing and rest. Strength is birthed from the pain we endure. Pain can force our focus to higher places. We must feel the pain before moving forward. Running a race with an injury exposed my pain, which began a long-awaited recovery—a recovery that reached every part of my being.

After the race, I told Jane about the discomfort I was still experiencing from my fall six weeks back. I was growing weary of the constant pain, the inability to lie down, and the effort it took to lift my arm. Jane owns her own physical therapy practice.

She is a gifted practitioner and graciously uses her gift of healing. After an extended time of analyzing my body, Jane encouraged me to get an x-ray.

I went to see a doctor nine weeks after my fall. The doctor asked why I had not come in earlier. She questioned how I could have run in a race. This was proof of the insanity I was living. I did not yet have an answer. She ordered an x-ray as a precaution—to rule out any broken ribs prior to beginning therapy.

I was brought to the x-ray room and told they might need to take several films. Broken ribs were often hard to see on an x-ray. I faced my most painful side to the camera. They shot the first two films. The technician went around the corner to view the results with the radiologist. A loud curse of disbelief came from around the corner. They both reentered the room and told me we were finished. The x-rays captured exactly what they needed. I was done within minutes of entering the room, something I had not expected.

I went back the following week to find out what the x-ray report revealed. The doctor said my injury was so severe that others viewing the films thought it was of an elderly patient with advanced osteoporosis. I had multiple transverse rib fractures. I am most certain there were more fractures in the other areas of similar pain I pointed out prior to the x-ray, but those were not filmed. Healing had barely started to take place after nine weeks. The doctor said it was imperative to rest and I was ordered to not bring further injury to these ribs. I had run a half marathon and finished the school year, five graduate classes, and a home-remodeling project with major injury. Summer never looked better.

> My grace is sufficient for you, for my power is made perfect in weakness. Therefore I will boast all the more gladly so that Christ's power may rest on me. That is why, for Christ's sake, delight in weaknesses, in insults, in hardships, in persecutions, in difficulties. For when I am weak, then I am strong.
> —2 Corinthians 12:9–10

Too much in life focuses on what we are *doing*. Some of the most important aspects of our life in Christ have nothing to do with what we *do* but rather *who we are*. Developing as a follower of Christ cannot happen if we are always doing. We need to understand what time it is—time to do or time to be. There is a time for everything—a time to run and a time to walk; a time to walk and a time to sit; a time to sit and a time to lie down; and a time to a lie down and a time to sleep.

A physical trainer once shared that time spent in recovery after a long run could equal the amount of time spent actually running. For example, an hour run could be backed up to an hour of stretching. This would produce the best recovery and ensure better overall physical outcomes. I wondered if anyone followed this advice. At the time, this strategy seemed impossible. Why was I so quick to want to dismiss it? My answer: I did not have the time. I had the time to run for an hour and a half, but five to ten minutes was all I was willing to give my body to recover. This was also reflected in how I lived life. I would go from one event to another. Project after project would begin like clockwork. Date after date was planned, leaving a calendar with no availability. Less and less sleep transpired to ensure every commitment was accomplished.

We are given a limited amount of resources in a lifetime. These resources need to be accounted for and used with wisdom. Our great-uncle Chuck once told Matt, "If you don't have the money to buy it, don't get it." The same is true about any resource we use in life. When we do not have the capability of using a resource without hurting another area in our life, we need to take a pass on using this resource or adjust the goal so it fits within our limits. Only on rare occasions should we consider extending beyond our resources, and this should be done only with wise council and prayer.

How many stresses do we put on ourselves by not evaluating our resources before executing our plans? We run at 110 percent, leaving no room for the unexpected. Margin must be calculated in our plan. Richard Swenson's book *Margin* states, "It is rare to see a life prescheduled to only eighty percent, leaving a margin for responding to the unexpected that God sends our way."[1] When we do not have a specific resource or are tapped out in every way, we are foolish to expect the best outcome. We settle for good, leaving the best just out of reach.

Suppose one of you wants to build a tower. Won't you first sit down and estimate the cost to see if you have enough money to

complete it? For if you lay the foundation and are not able to finish it, everyone who sees it will ridicule you, saying, "This person began to build and wasn't able to finish."
 —Luke 14:28–30

The diagnosis of multiple rib fractures limited my physical activity. My summer took on a completely new twist. The doctor ordered me to heal, and that is exactly what I did—for the first time in forty years. I sat. I rested. I wrote. I visited. I fished. I napped. I placed boundaries on my body to aid its healing.

Because of my limited ability for exercise, I allowed myself to experience yoga for the first time in life. Prior to this injury, I had never set foot inside a yoga studio. I feared yoga would challenge the strict disciplines to which I adhered.

We demolish arguments and every pretension that sets itself up against the knowledge of God, and we take captive every thought to make it obedient to Christ.
 —2 Corinthians 10:5

Therefore, my dear friends, as you have always obeyed—not only in my presence, but now much more in my absence—continue to work out your salvation with fear and trembling …
 —Philippians 2:12

Yoga is an ancient practice. For some, its meaning has shifted over the years, practicing only the physical benefits. Each instructor brings attention to different elements of the practice. The discipline of yoga unites the mind, body, and spirit. My yoga experience began in the tiny Wisconsin town of Egg Harbor.

Kathy was manning the checkout counter at a quaint specialty grocery store.[2] We began a short conversation as she packed my goods. It turned out that Kathy taught yoga in a barn just down the road from where I was staying. She invited me to check it out.

My brokenness kept me from most exercise. It was the end of May, and I could not lie on my back, roll over, or lift a glass with my right arm. The jostle of running ached. Planking, push-ups, and pull-ups were completely out of the question; therefore, I thought yoga was out of the question as well.

Kathy's yoga studio[3] piqued my interest. Later that same day, I visited her site. Kathy taught a restorative yoga class—gentle yoga focusing on small movements—the following morning. The class catered to seniors or individuals in physical recovery. I thought I might be able to do this. I knew, if nothing else, it would be fun to see where Kathy worked and hopefully create a connection for the future.

The following morning was picture-perfect. Wispy white clouds painted themselves against a sunny sapphire sky. Lilacs and other Wisconsin summer favorites were in full bloom. The wind had not yet awakened. With plenty of time to spare, I readied my bicycle for the day's transportation. I leisurely peddled passing views of abandoned farms, cow pastures, and alfalfa fields. Up and down rolling hills. The ride was picture perfect.

A gentleman, cutting some bushes near the parking lot, kindly greeted me upon arrival and pointed the way to the studio. I began the gentle walk up a path lined with wildflowers, roped lights, and metal art. Tall pines with exposed roots acted as a doorway at the end of the path, naturally leading to the barn. The barn left no clues as to if it was the yoga studio. I approached with caution, entered, and allowed the screen door to softly close. The room was dead quiet and not a soul in sight. This must have been the wrong entrance. I headed out and around back, where another window and door gave a view of the studio. I heard Kathy talking and saw movement. I headed toward the door to enter when something in the grass caught my attention. I looked down to find that I was straddling a mature fox snake. The snake stared straight at me, slowly rising with a slight hiss and rattle.

I screamed and jumped back. The quietness of the studio had been disturbed. Frightened and embarrassed, I ran around the other side of the barn and sat down. I pulled out my phone. It was five after ten. The class started at ten. I was late. As far I was concerned, this all meant no yoga for me today. I ran back to my bike, hopped on, secured my helmet, and peddled down the drive.

The gentleman I met earlier had now worked his way to the end of the drive fixing a pothole. He called out, "Did you find the studio?" I stopped upon reaching him and responded, "Yes, but I didn't realize how tardy I was. I didn't want to disrupt the flow, so I will just come back another day." He softly replied, "But you road *all* the way here. You had a goal in your mind and were so close to reaching it. You can't leave. You must go back. In fact, just this morning I wrote a quote about saying *yes*. There is no way you can leave without saying *yes* to the reason you came."

As a teacher, I am all about the bell, being on time, and being respectful to everyone in the class. Heading back to enter at a severely tardy state went against everything in my bones—especially since I did not have a clue as to what yoga entailed. But, there I went, heading back up the same grassy path I had walked fifteen minutes earlier. I took a deep breath, grasped the correct door handle this time, and entered a quiet studio. Everyone was in pose. I chose a space on the floor and arranged my mat.

Because of my state of mind it took a couple minutes to realize that an injured dog lay on a pillow next to me. He was so still. I would have definitely chosen another seat had I been more aware. His body was shaven and stapled from head to paw. He wore an oversized T-shirt. After my initial inspection, I smiled. So random yet appropriate. I was to experience my first yoga class next to another injured being.

Kathy acknowledged me within seconds. She called me by name, got equipment for me, and helped with positions. Fear of performing was nonexistent. Everyone was at a different level, and Kathy instructed as such. This was the first of many sessions. Healing began immediately. I gained movement and strength. Pain subsided.

Kathy's warm-up sessions brought us to the extreme present, leaving zero room for the past or future. My mind delighted in God's creation as we were instructed to focus on all of our senses, one at a time. I was able to relax. My mind was still for the first time in decades. My thoughts were fully centered on the only moment God had given me—the present.

Fear of the past, fear of the future, and people-pleasing tend to be the cause of much anxiety. When our minds are focused on the present, anxiety struggles to exist. Living in the present is the only place I can give God glory, as it is the only place I exist. We give our attention to the present when the past and future are shut off.

The concept of walking one minute after every mile can only take place if we are aware of the present—aware of what is going on around us, how we are feeling, and how others are feeling. I am beginning to hear my conscience saying, "Jo, you've run a mile. It is time to walk for a minute." I am slowly recognizing this voice and surrendering whatever I am doing at the time. Walking one minute after every mile is about regularly taking my eyes off the horizontals of life and getting them fixed up vertically on the eternal. It is about surrendering my agenda for God's agenda. It is about trusting that God is in control, even when the circumstances before me say something else. It is about working hard six days a week and leaving the seventh for rest.

Observe the Sabbath, because it is holy to you. Anyone who desecrates it is to be put to death; those who do any work on that day must be cut off from their people. For six days work is to be done, but the seventh day is a day of Sabbath rest, holy to the Lord. Whoever does any work on the Sabbath day is to be put

to death. The Israelites are to observe the Sabbath, celebrating it for the generations to come as a lasting covenant. It will be a sign between me and the Israelites forever, for in six days the Lord made the heavens and the earth, and on the seventh day he rested and was refreshed.
    —Exodus 31:14–17

He says, "Be still, and know that I am God; I will be exalted among the nations, I will be exalted in the earth."
    —Psalm 46:10

Let everything that has breath praise the Lord.
Praise the Lord.
    —Psalm 150:6

He makes me lie down in green pastures, he leads me beside quiet waters, he refreshes my soul. He guides me along the right paths for his name's sake.
    —Psalm 23:1–4

Come to me, all you who are weary and burdened, and I will give you rest …
    —Matthew 11:28

    The broken need rest. But healing does not stop with the broken. Just as the health world speaks of free radicals bombarding our cells with constant determination, so the world and our daily routines damage our physical, emotional, and spiritual beings. We all are in need of healing, whether we consider ourselves broken or not. Healing is a process God wants us to take seriously. Sabbath rest, praising him consistently throughout the day, prayer, meditation on the Word, and allowing others to share our burdens are all ways Scripture allows for daily, weekly, and monthly healing.

Allowing ourselves to heal and become whole brings many benefits. We are recharged, focused, and able to use our gifts of ministry to glorify God. Our minds are given a place to rest, focusing our eyes back on God, whom we can trust. In addition, others are served, as we have strength and margin to serve them.

One of the greatest commands in the Bible is to love our neighbor as ourselves. If we do not know how to care for ourselves, it will be impossible to care for others. Understanding what my needs are and meeting them is loving and will ultimately help me understand the needs of others. I need time to rest, recharge, and spend with the Lord. I begin to deteriorate emotionally, physically, and spiritually when busyness creeps in. I drag when my week is devoid of Sabbath. Love goes out the window, and bitterness, anger, and depression seeps in.

We must strive for healing on a daily basis—or better yet, moment by moment. A true understanding of our feeble condition as humans and our utmost dependence on our maker should bring our longing for restoration. God sent Jesus to bring abundance to our lives that can only be fulfilled through him. Healing, restoration, and getting recharged can only take place when we are connected to the source of life.

Finally, brothers and sisters, rejoice! Strive for full restoration, encourage one another, be of one mind, live in peace. And the God of love and peace will be with you.
—2 Corinthians 13:11–13

The thief comes only to steal and kill and destroy; I have come that they may have life, and have it to the full.
—John 10:10

Abide in me, and I in you. As the branch cannot bear fruit by itself, unless it abides in the vine, neither can you, unless you abide in me.
—John 15:4 ESV

Abundance is found in the life that has been restored through living in the presence of God Almighty. The most powerful image a Christian can witness is the restoration of another person's life. Our church regularly shares videos of God at work in the lives of people from our own congregation.[4] I have yet to make it through one of these videos with dry eyes. Why the tears? Restoration of a person by Jesus Christ is an eternal event. This person has crossed over from the death of Eden to the resurrection of Easter's tomb. He or she has tapped in to the eternal answer of all answers, the joy of all joys, the comfort of all comforts, the peace of all peace, the provider of all providers. No money, labor, or acts of kindness could secure this. It is the faith of a child, the complete trust, and the surrender of one's life that brings about eternal restoration.

God creates a picture of restoration through his creation. Several years ago, a mighty storm came through our village of Lombard—trees torn in two, power lines left hanging, and shingles scattered across front yards. Our home survived the storm. My favorite old gnarly maple tree was another story. It had graced our backyard by holding a perfectly thick, round canopy, home to a wide variety of critters. Not anymore. It was completely ripped in half, crushing our sweet wooden swing below. My heart sank. I had little hope of the tree's survival. After sawing away the fallen half, I applied tar to the large open wound left in the bark. I would have to wait to see if it would continue to thrive.

A year passed, and the tree hung on. Its canopy was sparse and its trunk distorted from the ragged ripping away of the fallen half. Year after year, it continued on with life. This past summer, I noticed something I had never stopped to study. Over the years, the tree had been going through a slow restoration. A large, thick bark scab had evolved around the tear in its side. The original splintered tear could barely be seen. The tree's canopy now stretched over the portion lost seven years earlier. Even though the bark scab would never bring the tree back to its original state, it was necessary for it to form. The scab helped the tree withstand the elements, disease, and pests. Had it not formed, the tree would have been weakened and susceptible. Instead, it continued to thrive and once again produces a beautiful canopy of leaves.

I felt like this tree. I was weak, worn, and broken after the storm I passed through in the last months. My pain and x-ray were evidence that healing was barely beginning. I had to be still, like this tree. Time had to pass to heal the brokenness. Serving others in need, being productive in my home, and exercise had to be put on hold. Continued activity of any kind would jeopardize my bones from growing back together. My heart and mind were also broken. These too needed to be still, like the tree, patiently allowing the scab to form. Restoration does not come on its own. It is revealed through a mind that understands who God is, a life willing to put God in the place of authority, and a heart that trusts God implicitly and brings glory to him, regardless of the circumstances.

Though the fig tree does not bud and there are no grapes on the vines, though the olive crop fails and the fields produce no food, though there are no sheep in the pen and no cattle in the stalls, yet I will rejoice in the Lord, I will be joyful in God my Savior. The Sovereign Lord is my strength; he makes my feet like the feet of a deer, he enables me to tread on the heights."
—Habakkuk 3:17–19

Being still is a hard task for someone always on the go. God knew I would need help with this and paired me with a husband who knows how to be still. Matt is patient and always full of joy. I can wake him at the crack of dawn and he faces me with a squinted smile. He whistles cheery tunes while working. He always has time to listen or snuggle. Matt is 100 percent "Mary," married to one of the biggest "Marthas" around.

As Jesus and his disciples were on their way, he came to a village where a woman named Martha opened her home to him. She had a sister called Mary, who sat at the Lord's feet listening to what he

said. But Martha was distracted by all the preparations that had to be made. She came to him and asked, "Lord, don't you care that my sister has left me to do the work by myself? Tell her to help me!" "Martha, Martha," the Lord answered, "you are worried and upset about many things, but few things are needed—or indeed only one. Mary has chosen what is better, and it will not be taken away from her."
 —Luke 10:38–42

When I want to light a fire under Matt, he is thinking about dumping a bucket of ice on my head. I say this with a smile. We are blessed by each other's differences. Embracing our personal character traits as God's handiwork makes our marriage whole. Matt is balm to my spirit; he aids in my healing and encourages rest and rejuvenation.

Love, joy, peace, patience, kindness, goodness, faithfulness, gentleness, and self-control—they are called the fruits of the Spirit and are found in the book of Galatians.[5] I long to have them in my life. They are posted on the walls of our home. They serve as a reminder of how far my actual life is from attaining them. That is the point; I cannot access these fruits by myself. They are the result of the Spirit's control of my life.

I trump Matt when it comes to time spent on spiritual disciplines—hours of Bible study, Scripture memorization, prayer, and service to others. So why does Matt so easily demonstrate the fruit of the Spirit while I fail? The biggest difference in our lives is that Matt has margin. He takes time for restoration. He puts aside work. It took me forty years of life to realize that the life

Matt leads is what I need. He gives himself a Sabbath every week. He ensures one day of rest and then works hard on the other days. He thoughtfully plans what is on his plate seven days a week. He understands what it means to walk one minute after every mile.

    I am an over-functioner. My decisions are made out of fear, rather than focusing on God. I need boundaries in place to help me function at the pace God intended. I want to place God at the center of all my work and step away from impressing others. I want my love for him to be the fuel that fills the desire to serve others. I want to sit at his feet, putting aside the busyness of life. These desires, put into action, prevent running at a ragged pace. We offer our bodies as a sacrifice, but God never meant that we were to forget our own health while doing it.

Therefore, I urge you, brothers and sisters, in view of God's mercy, to offer your bodies as a living sacrifice, holy and pleasing to God—this is your true and proper worship. Do not conform to the pattern of this world, but be transformed by the renewing of your mind. Then you will be able to test and approve what God's will is—his good, pleasing and perfect will.
    —Romans 12:1–2

For my yoke is easy and my burden is light.
    —Matthew 11:30

    I thank God that Matt has never wanted to keep up with me. He is an example of someone who functions at a healthy pace. He is rarely worn out and runs life at a consistent speed. He has time for refueling—physically, emotionally, and spiritually. He always has space to serve others. It is his pace that fosters the love, joy, peace, patience, kindness, goodness, faithfulness, gentleness, and self-control he shares with others. It is his intentional breaks and focus on God that allow for healing in all areas of his life. It is his faith of being sure of what he hopes for that allows him to set aside life's agenda and rest.

Stop and Abide

Relax

Gratitude trumps anxiety. Being thankful for God's blessings wipes away stress and anxiety. Begin a regular habit of thanking God. It could be in your head, on your phone, a text to a friend, or in a journal. Right now, list three or more blessings. This should be an ongoing exercise done from the moment your eyes open to right before they close at the end of the day. When anxiety begins to seep in, combat it with thankfulness. When you are stressed, meditate on your list of blessings.

"Let the peace of Christ rule in your hearts, since as members of one body you were called to peace. And be thankful" (Colossians 3:15).

Reflect

- What is the purpose of pain?
  (Proverbs 3:5–8; 2 Corinthians 12:7–10; 1 Peter 5:6–11)

- What needs to change in your life so that abiding with God becomes a reality? (Romans 13:12–14; Hebrews 11:6; James 4:8)

- How can you offer your body as a living sacrifice to God? (Romans 12:1–2; 1 Peter 2:4–5)

_____

_____

_____

_____

_____

Jo Anna Rieger

Eyes Up

Ashamed of ... *neglect, selfishness, exhaustion, conceit*

You are ... *holy, righteous, just, true*

Blessed by ... *suffering, sacrifice, redemption, healing*

Please ... *strengthen, prompt, perfect, pursue*

Amen

9

Finish

> However, I consider my life worth nothing to me;
> my only aim is to finish the race and complete the task
> the Lord Jesus has given me—the task of testifying to
> the good news of God's grace.
> —Acts 20:24

The finish line is the goal of a runner, just as heaven is the goal of a Christian. Finishing life's race well is critical, as crossing the line will bring every person before the throne of God. How runners look when they cross the line exposes their purpose and strategies for running. The same is true of how Christians look when they cross over into eternity. Christians finish the race well by completing the tasks to which God called them. It is imperative to consider the end of the race long before the finish line is in sight. Ensuring a strong finish begins now.

Definition of Abide

[*uh*-bahyd]

Verb (used without object), abode or abided, abiding.
1. to remain; continue; stay:
2. to have one's abode; dwell; reside:
3. to continue in a particular condition, attitude, relationship.[1]

Abiding with God throughout the race is the key for finishing well. Abiding is constant. It never stops. It takes rejecting Satan's lies, surrendering to God, giving up striving in our own strength, and realigning our lives to Christ. To abide is to stay plugged into our source. The minute we unplug is the minute we begin traveling down our own faulty, self-centered, people-pleasing, fear-driven ways.

Jeff Donaldson is a pastor in our church. He is passionate for the Word and humble in sharing his shortcomings. He has a gift of making Scripture understandable, making him a great teacher. Jeff does this by touching the heart and engaging the mind with the use of metaphor. Although it has been years since his sermon on abiding, an image he used has stayed with me. Right in the middle of a sermon, Jeff entered an already erected tent, slid his legs through two pre-cut holes in its floor, lifted the tent, and began to walk around the stage preaching his message on abiding. This was his illustration of what it meant to abide with God.

This visual example outlines a strong sense of commitment—staying, dwelling, remaining, continuing. Like grapes to a vine is the runner who abides in Jesus Christ. To have a successful run in the Christian life, it is imperative to commit to abiding.

The following versions of John 15:4 describe the importance of abiding:

> Abide in me, and I in you. As the branch cannot bear fruit by itself, unless it abides in the vine, neither can you, unless you abide in me. ESV

> Stay joined to me, and I will stay joined to you. Just as a branch cannot produce fruit unless it stays joined to the vine, you cannot produce fruit unless you stay joined to me. CEV

> Remain in me, as I also remain in you. No branch can bear fruit by itself; it must remain in the vine. Neither can you bear fruit unless you remain in me. NIV

A successful race on earth depends on how much we are connected to Jesus Christ, the source of everything we need. He is our coach. He plans the race. He sets our pace. He provides the best gear. He fills our cup at each mile. He walks with us up the hardest hills. He cheers us on at the finish line. He restores us after the race. He provides it all. Why do we think we can make it through life without fully submitting to him? Why would we want to?

Abiding with Jesus Christ ceases when I

- wake up in the morning without praising God.
- attack problems in my own strength.
- refuse the need for a day of rest.
- prioritize my to-do list over people.
- do not put God on my daily schedule.
- feel the need to control.
- enter a new year without a plan for abiding.

God takes what we are learning and provides opportunity for practice. Prior to starting the school year, I uttered a prayer. I asked God to help keep my mind fixed on the eternal in the midst of the mundane. It had been a summer of restoration, and I wanted to make sure it continued as I went back to work. I had developed some harmful habits over the last nineteen years of teaching. I needed God's help to slow down, take on less, and focus on seeing him in the midst of a busy day.

God sent an "angel" to help with exactly what I asked him for. Angel, a fifth year senior in my art class, was new to our department. His purpose for taking the class was to get a credit with the least amount of effort possible so he could get out of high school. His interest in art was zero. He was gifted in communication and negotiation. I had my work cut out.

My agenda for the third day of class included an entertaining clip of art history. It was the foundation of the day's lesson. I ensured the clip was ready to play for the day. It performed flawlessly for my first two classes. When it came time to play the clip for Angel's class, all that was heard from the speakers was a choppy, crackled sound. The video image moved one frame every couple of seconds. I immediately went into computer-technologist mode. Frantic as student conversations began to take over the class, I rechecked multiple connections. I refreshed the video. Nothing. I was about to try yet another option, when out from the student audience I was reminded to stop and abide. Angel had sat silently through this whole episode. He had watched me carefully and could not hold back any longer. "Mrs. Rieger, maybe God doesn't want you to play that video to our class right now."

I froze in my tracks. Did a student just bring God into our classroom? He sure did and there was the answer to my prayer. Angel was right. Why did I fight this and create such unrest in my class by trying to overpower the inevitable? I looked at Angel, affirmed his conclusion, and class went on. It was not until evening that I truly realized what had happened in class. God spoke through an angel to get my attention in the middle of a chaotic episode. Striving to abide brings God into every avenue of your day.

The finish line exposes a runner's race. How a runner crosses the line tells what happened during the race. How we abide with God will be evident at our heavenly finish line. The most profound detail of the Door County Half Marathon was my time at the end of the race. It was evident that I *had* abided with Tim, our pacer.

When running a race, runners receive an electronic chip that calculates the runner's actual time. The chip is activated upon crossing the start line and then deactivated when crossing the finish line. This time is called the "chip time" and is different from what the clock time projects at the start and finish line. Only a handful of runners can cross the start line at the same time. With thousands of participants in a race, the chip creates a way to calculate each runner's time. The chip time is the runner's real race time and can be gathered at the result tent at the end of a race or on the official race website.

A day after the Door County Half Marathon, I logged in to the race website to find out my chip time. I was confused. The time by my name read 2:15:00. Tim, our pacer, held up a flag during the race with the time of 2:15:00. This represented the pace he committed to run with the team. But how did the race coordinators know I was running with this pace team? Did Jane share this information with them? I figured I would look up Jane's time, thinking it would also read 2:15:00. This was a smaller race venue; thus, the actual chip times were possibly not available yet.

I got a surprise when Jane's time came up on the screen. Her time read 2:18:33 and not the 2:15:00 I had expected. This could mean only one thing: this *was* her actual chip time. Could it be that my time was exactly two hours and fifteen minutes, with no seconds before or after? Yep! That is exactly what that meant!

My chip time, although twenty four percent longer than my last half marathon, was incredible! It was 100 percent confirmation that this was more than just another race. I ran watch-less and broken yet ended spot on. I had let go and had committed to follow Tim, our 2:15 pacer from Appleton—the pacer who ran with an analog watch, walked one minute after ever mile, walked all hills, lost his team due to a bathroom stop, and then told us to run all out during our last mile. To hit 2:15:00 on the nose, with all the variables of this race, was a miracle. This was the knock in the head that opened my heart to hear God's message: "Stop and abide!"

Shortly after the Door County Half Marathon, I was able to partake in another race, the annual Chicago Half Marathon.[2] However, it was from the perspective of a volunteer. Matt and I were blessed to walk alongside Mitchell Swaback Charities,[3] an organization that takes their race in life seriously. I have run this very race with them in the past. In fact, my very first half marathon was run with MSC. I knew my body was still in need of rest; thus, I helped fill their quota for race volunteers instead. My job was to offer runners a bottle of water at the end of the race.

I stood in the same place for three hours, handing out water. Thousands passed by as I stood at their goal—the finish line, the place that marked the end of their pursuit. Volunteering for a pretty mindless task left room to reflect on the sea of runners passing by. Some passed with a smile. Others stumbled by emotionless. My mind sorted the runners into categories that began to naturally emerge: the strong, the thankful, the injured, and the untouched. I then began to imagine that the constructed finish line arch was actually heaven's gates. These runners were crossing their final finish line ever. This was it. An eternity lay before them.

The Strong

These were the runners who stood tall after crossing the line, smiled, and continued on to hug family at the sidelines. They strutted past me and grabbed for a bottle of water in each hand. No limps, no athletic tape, no drama—just a strong race with a strong finish. Many of these runners turned around and cheered on their friends as they crossed. These runners were ready for their medals and the party tent. Training, healing, and pacing had all been a part of these runners' lives for the last couple of months—and possibly years. This is how I want to look when crossing over into eternity—years of abiding, worshiping, and serving God all evident in how I end the race.

I have fought the good fight, I have finished the race, I have kept the faith.
 —2 Timothy 4:7

The Thankful

There were only a handful of "the Thankful." Every time one walked by, I snapped out of my rote job and passed off a big smile. The majority of these runners also belonged to the Strong category. What placed them in this category was the simple phrase, "Thank you for volunteering." My spirit was tickled each time I heard those words. Many of these runners had run for ninety or more minutes, and the first words to exit their mouths were "thank you."

Prior to this experience, I always envisioned crossing into heaven as a time when I would be welcomed home. In reality, I should be on my face, kissing the feet of Jesus, thanking him. Crossing the line into heaven will have absolutely nothing to do with me. It will have nothing to do with how I trained, stretched, ate, or paced. The only reason I will get to cross into heaven is because of the love of God, sending to earth his only guiltless Son, who died a horrific death by crucifixion, so I could one day spend eternity with him. How I long to fully understand what God did for me and to be a part of "the Thankful."

Do you see this woman? I came into your house. You did not give me any water for my feet, but she wet my feet with her tears and wiped them with her hair. You did not give me a kiss, but this woman, from the time I entered, has not stopped kissing my feet. You did not put oil on my head, but she has poured perfume on my feet. Therefore, I tell you, her many sins have been forgiven—as her great love has shown. But whoever has been forgiven little loves little.
—Luke 7:44–47

The Injured

There were taped knees, taped calves, taped thighs, limps, moans, wheelchairs, stretchers, and ice. Pain was about all these runners could focus on. I wondered how long they had been suffering. Did they begin the race with an injury? Did it happen somewhere on the route? Did it happen because of a lack of training? Lack of proper pacing? Was there any way they could have avoided it? Would walking one minute after every mile have helped some of these runners? This is not the way we are encouraged to end life's race.

Then there were those who crossed the line, exhausted. These were the runners who ran all out for the entire race, barely crossing the line and ending in a dramatic collapse. Some were held up by friends on each side. Others lay alone on the ground, while others were whisked away by race medics. These runners were wiped out. Many of them vomited. The party tent was the last thing on their minds. Such an uneventful way to cross the finish line, like lighting a bottle rocket that just fizzles out. Not the way I want to enter heaven.

I would like to learn just one thing from you: Did you receive the Spirit by the works of the law, or by believing what you heard? Are you so foolish? After beginning by means of the Spirit, are you now trying to finish by means of the flesh? Have you experienced so much in vain—if it really was in vain?
—Galatians 3:2

Do not offer to the Lord the blind, the injured or the maimed, or anything with warts or festering or running sores. Do not place any of these on the altar as a food offering presented to the Lord.
—Leviticus 22:22

"The Injured" describes Christians who run the race according to their own ways. They reject what God has prescribed in Scripture for a burdenless, abundant life. These runners trust in themselves and their own efforts. They are often busy doing good works in the church, yet their hearts are heavy and far from God. It is easy to describe the Injured, as they are a picture of where I was and could easily fall back to if I neglect abiding with God.

The Untouched

These runners had me stumped for a bit. I am almost positive that their heartbeats did not leave the resting zone. Hairdos remained untouched and makeup unblemished, ready for a night out on the town. Evidence of sweat was nonexistent. Did they even try to walk quickly? Was their goal to look better when they finished than when they started? Were they worried about how they would *look* in their official race photos? This is not what I mean about finishing well. Just because runners look great does not mean they ran well.

I began to imagine how these runners would look in the spiritual world. Could they be likened to the servant who was given a bag of money and buried it, returning it to his master with no interest? This servant was called wicked and lazy. What drove the servant to be cast away by the master? It began by a fear of failing. Was fear the reason these runners did not try?

Then the man who had received one bag of gold came. "Master," he said, "I knew that you are a hard man, harvesting where you have not sown and gathering where you have not scattered seed. So I was afraid and went out and hid your gold in the ground. See, here is what belongs to you." His master replied, "You wicked,

lazy servant! So you knew that I harvest where I have not sown and gather where I have not scattered seed? Well then, you should have put my money on deposit with the bankers, so that when I returned I would have received it back with interest."
—Matthew 25:24–27

Or maybe the Untouched could be likened to the hypocrites Jesus described in Mathew 23. These runners look great from the outside—they have all the latest gear, spend hours reading about nutrition, and even have a lifetime membership to the most prestigious gym in town—but their hearts and bodies show no evidence of health. It is all a show, and their race will never be run well.

Woe to you, teachers of the law and Pharisees, you hypocrites! You are like whitewashed tombs, which look beautiful on the outside but on the inside are full of the bones of the dead and everything unclean. In the same way, on the outside you appear to people as righteous but on the inside you are full of hypocrisy and wickedness. Whatever the case, may this description never be you. Our resources are God given. They are intended to be used to build the Church. It is a fearful thing to fall into the hands of a Master in which we squandered what was given.
—Matthew 23:27–28

Todd Boyd, Matt's best friend, finished his "race" strong. Todd was forty-eight years old, with no sign that he would be crossing the line on that summer morning. It just happened. Unlike the mile markers on a real race, many of us do not know when life's race will end. There were no crowds cheering Todd in the seconds before he died. No medals being placed around his neck. No chip times to look up. At least, none of this from our perspective here on earth.

Todd was a best friend to many. He was also Matt's small-group leader and number-one encourager. Matt's cell phone regularly chimed well before sunrise. It was Todd, sharpening the men in his life with a verse for the day. His famous quote, based on a men's retreat they attended, was, "Act like men!"[4] Todd cared for more people than anyone will ever know. On the same day that he underwent medical testing and his wife was put in the hospital, Todd made his way to our home to plow me out of a blizzard. His life was built on two principles: loving God and loving people. He accomplished these well.

I cannot help but think that there were crowds cheering Todd on as he entered eternity—those who knew him and already had finished their races, along with choirs of angels. Instead of a cheap race medal, Todd was given an eternal crown. Instead of a chip time, his entire track record of life was reviewed. It was said by many of his family and friends that Todd heard, "Well done, good and faithful servant!"[5] Story after story was shared at Todd's memorial service of how he touched and brought the light of Christ to others. Todd's trust in Jesus Christ was obvious to others. His daily submission to God's Word guided his race. His memorial shared his favorite verse:

Trust in the LORD with all your heart and lean not on your own understanding; in all your ways submit to him, and he will make your paths straight.
—Proverbs 3:5–6

Trust and submission are major components in walking one minute after every mile. For the Door County Half Marathon, thanks to a wise friend, I committed to a specific finish time, found someone I trusted to get me there, followed his lead the whole way, and submitted to his strategies. My result? Crossing the finish line at the exact time I committed to at the beginning of the race. Is this how it could be when we close our eyes for the last time if we commit ourselves to God's way for our life?

Therefore, since we are surrounded by such a great cloud of witnesses, let us throw off everything that hinders and the sin that so easily entangles. And let us run with perseverance the race marked out for us, fixing our eyes on Jesus, the pioneer and perfecter of faith.
—Hebrews 12:1–2a

June 1988 marked my graduation from Timothy Christian Junior High. Our class verse for that day was none other than Hebrews 12:1–2. June 1992 marked my high school graduation from Timothy Christian High School. I am not sure if this verse was linked to our class, but the front cover of our graduation program read Hebrews 12:1–2. And then came freshman orientation at Wheaton College. Was it coincidence that Hebrews 12:1–2 was chosen as our freshman class verse? I can still hear the tune that the freshmen orientation committee composed to accompany our class verse. There we stood on Edmund Chapel's stage, united as college freshman, singing out our class verse. It went something like this:

> There—for, since we are surrounded
> By such a great cloud—of witnesses
> Let us throw off everything that hinders us
> And the sin that so easily entangles us
> And let us run with perseverance
> The race marked out for us
>
> [Guys] Let us fix our eyes
> [Girls] Let us fix our eyes
> [Guys] Let us fix our eyes
> [Girls] Let us fix our eyes
> [All] Let us fix our eyes on Jesus
> He will perfect our faith

Putting words to a tune solidifies them in our souls for life. It is well over twenty years since I was a freshman at Wheaton College, yet, there is not a word of Hebrews 12:1-2 that I have forgotten. That may be the reason this verse has become so ingrained in all I do. It is a powerful Scripture that also became our wedding verse; it is hung in my office; and it underlies how I often encourage others. I have a habit of signing letters with "Eyes Up!"

The first portion of this passage charges us to look around at our great witnesses. Some have crossed the finish line, such as Todd. Others are nearing it. Some are in the middle of the race.

Some have just begun. We are told that it is because of these witnesses that we are supposed to run well. Todd's dedication, perseverance, and testimony have helped so many reevaluate how they have been running, me included. His witness of Jesus Christ has challenged me to turn over a new leaf. Biographies of people such as Dietrich Bonhoeffer, Hudson Taylor, and Amy Carmichael are more witnesses that have sharpened my faith and challenged me to a move to a new level. And then I have my "sisters"—the cluster of women with whom I do life. They encourage me, ask the hard questions, and give wise counsel. All around us are earthly models, who not only have witnessed the awesomeness of God, but also have made obedience to Jesus Christ their highest calling. They will be the ones who give us the support to stay strong to the end.

Once we take inventory of our surrounding witnesses, Hebrews 12 instructs us to throw off everything that hinders and entangles. Outside of running, Matt and I hike and climb. Our first time out West together was in 1998. Those first summits, compared to some of our most recent, differ significantly in what gear we were willing to carry. Years of experience helped shave off what was not necessary and considered luxury. Unnecessary gear slows the climber down, wears on the body, and may even add danger.

In 2000, Matt and I set out to summit Mount Moran, a 12,605-foot mountain located in Grand Teton National Park.[6] Leaving hours before sunrise, the trip began with canoeing across a glacial lake, a short portage, and then another paddle to the base of the mountain. After stashing the canoe, we loaded packs onto our backs, adjusted hiking poles, and began our ascent up the mountain. Our packs held two sixty-meter ropes, two harnesses, two helmets, two sets of climbing shoes, a full set of traditional climbing gear, a tent, two sleeping bags, food, a stove, a cooking pot, clothing, camp suds, and rain gear. Each step was up. Our footing juggled between rocks and giant boulders. I kept thinking how much more enjoyable it would be if I did not have all the gear on my back. It took hours to get up to base camp; a day was left for climbing to the summit, and a day to get back down. It was physically brutal and extremely slow-going.

Eleven years later, we had a 1:30 a.m. arrival at the Long's Peak trailhead, a 14,259-foot mountain located in Rocky Mountain National Park.[7] We planned to summit and make it back to our car before 1:00 p.m. to miss the afternoon rainstorms. We enjoyed a breathtaking sunrise, a careful climb through the keyhole route, a relaxing lunch on the summit, and still made it back to our car a little after noon. It was an enjoyable challenge.

As we passed a base camp along the way, I was reminded of our Mount Moran endeavor and began to compare the two. What was the difference? Our plan did not involve camping or technical climbing. These were options we could have taken but chose not to do. This did not affect summiting. We probably made it to the summit in half the time by taking a different route than the technical climbers. We threw off anything we did not need for the journey. It was fun. It was fulfilling. We have photos of this trip going all the way up.

When I tried to find photos going up Mount Moran, all I could find was one photo of the place where my foot got stuck between rocks on a creek—not the best moment or one I would choose to remember. Frustration was the main feeling that marked this adventure.

As for Long's Peak, we enjoyed the climb from the beginning to the end. We stopped often to take photos. It was an inspirational climb. We worked together as a team with little to no frustration. I carried a small backpack with my water, rain gear, coat, and gloves. Matt's pack carried some protein bars, dried fruit, a first-aid kit, rain gear, safety rope, and coat. What we carried was a fraction of what we needed to ascend Mount Moran. Our strategy for summiting a mountain had changed. We still summit some amazing mountains, but we make sure to choose only those we can access in a day's time—this limits what we have to carry. This has revolutionized our hiking, making it such a pleasurable experience in so many ways. We still go rock climbing, but that is all we do for the day and make sure access to the route can be reached within an hour or less. This makes for a great day of climbing and a great night, as we are within close distance of a shower, bed, and good food.

Throwing off the hindrances and entanglements in our run for life will do exactly the same thing. Our run will become freer and clearer as distractions and desires are placed aside for a better run. By stripping down to the basics of our needs, we may avoid getting entangled by busyness and pleasing others. The "finish line" becomes our clear goal and all plans involve making it here safely, successfully, and abundantly. We are willing to sacrifice comfort as we look forward into eternity.

Through whom we have gained access by faith into this grace in which we now stand. And we boast in the hope of the glory of God. Not only so, but we also glory in our sufferings, because we know that suffering produces perseverance; perseverance, character; and character, hope.
—Romans 5:2–4

Because you know that the testing of your faith produces perseverance. Let perseverance finish its work so that you may be mature and complete, not lacking anything. If any of you lacks wisdom, you should ask God, who gives generously to all without finding fault, and it will be given to you.
—James 1:3–5

By throwing off everything that hinders, running with perseverance becomes much easier. Running with perseverance is different from running to finish. Perseverance requires urgency and determination. There is a pursuit of the goal without any wavering. Every second is accounted for.

A Christian who runs with perseverance

- believes the Bible is God's Word.
- loves others deeply.
- loves God even more deeply.
- understands the finish line is right around the corner.
- knows we are accountable to God.
- has a plan and adheres to it.

It is fitting that the author of Hebrews immediately puts "fix our eyes on Jesus" right after "run with perseverance." In order to run with perseverance, runners need to know their goals. Our final goal, as Christians, is to be in eternity with Jesus. By fixing our eyes on him throughout our race on earth, we are aligning our hearts and minds to our purpose and goal.

"Jesus is my pacer"—this phrase was created by my friend Julie. She was up in Wisconsin on the same weekend of the Door County Half Marathon. We were able to have dinner the night after the race. As a sister in Christ, I was excited to share the spiritual lessons I had learned from the race. Julie immediately saw the parallels between Christ and a pacer. When we fix our eyes on Jesus, we are putting the results of life's endeavors in his hands. We are trusting that he knows exactly how to pace us. We believe he is experienced in running the race and has the best intentions for us. When our eyes are focused on the pacer and not the circumstances around us, we are able to focus our energies on just following.

Running with a pacer is so different from running alone. When I run alone, my focus is on the time, my heart rate, mile markers, strategies, and passing other runners. My head is working as hard as the rest of my body. This is so true of how I live my life when Jesus Christ is not my ultimate focus. I focus on everything around me. The tasks of life become so big. I begin to strategize. My pace starts to fluctuate as injuries become evident. My thoughts become clogged. Not until I break down, get on my knees, and surrender my situation to God am I able to get back up and get back in the race, this time fixing my eyes on my pacer.

Jesus is the perfecter of my faith! Thank goodness, because when I begin to dig deep, the whole faith thing honestly hurts my head. There are times we have to let go and trust as a child trusts. Faith is not something I can concoct. It is God at work in me that does the concocting. God is willing to work if I am willing to get out of the way.

Let us never become distracted by all the great witnesses around us. Too often, we become addicted to God's people and their blogs, tweets, books, or podcasts. We follow people instead of following Christ. Jesus is our number-one example. Focusing on his life throughout Scripture is the solution to success in our own runs.

"However, I consider my life worth nothing to me; my only aim is to finish the race and complete the task the Lord Jesus has given me—the task of testifying to the good news of God's grace."
—Acts 20:24

We can count on running well, on pace, and without regret when we surrender our lives to Jesus Christ, abiding with him continually. Take up the techniques shared in each chapter and your run will never be the same. When you breathe your last, you will cross the finish line with strength, able to lay down your crown at the foot of the one who had everything to do with your race run well.

> Whenever the living creatures give glory, honor and thanks to him who sits on the throne and who lives for ever and ever, the twenty-four elders fall down before him who sits on the throne and worship him who lives for ever and ever. They lay their crowns before the throne and say:
>
> "You are worthy, our Lord and God, to receive glory and honor and power, for you created all things, and by your will they were created and have their being."
>
> —Revelation 4:9–11

Stop and Abide

Relax

Many runners schedule a massage upon completion of a race. It is a time scheduled for rest and recovery. Touch is found throughout Scripture and is often connected with healing. Massage is a way to bring healing to your overworked, stressed-out body. It releases anxiety and has been shown to reduce a multitude of physical ailments.

If a massage is not something you are able to schedule in this season of life, a mini-massage has similar benefits. Start by massaging your left hand with the right hand. Rub in a circular motion. Squeeze every finger. Continue by making your way up the left arm, and then come back down. Repeat on the other hand and arm. Next, move to your head. Closing your eyes will make this more relaxing. Move your index and middle fingers in small, gentle circles. Follow a line from your temple, up your hairline, down your forehead, across your eyebrows, and then back to your temples. Give your shoulders some gentle rubs and squeezes. Lastly, take a long breath in and out.

"Therefore, since we have these promises, dear friends, let us purify ourselves from everything that contaminates body and spirit, perfecting holiness out of reverence for God" (2 Corinthians 7:1).

Reflect

- How will you ensure that you will not be labeled the "lazy servant"? (Matthew 25:26–30)

- What do you want others to say about you at your memorial service? (Matthew 25:21)

- How are you going to ensure that you run well all the way to heaven's finish line? (Psalm 125:1; John 15:4–5; 1 John 2:28)

Eyes Up

Ashamed of ... *hiding, striving, forgetting, forfeiting*

You are ... *perfect, gentle, powerful, exalted*

Blessed by ... *faith, family, inadequacies, eternity*

Please ... *instill, convict, fill, carry*

Amen

Notes

Preface

1. *Door County Half Marathon and Nicolet Bay 5K*, accessed July 1, 2014, http://www.doorcountyhalfmarathon.com.

2. "Run Walk Run," *Jeff Galloway Official Website*, accessed July 4, 2014, http://www.jeffgalloway.com/training/run-walk.

3. Richard Swenson, *Margin: Restoring Emotional, Physical, Financial, and Time Reserves to Overloaded Lives* (Colorado Springs: NavPress, 2004), back cover.

4. Oswald Chambers, *My Utmost for His Highest* (New York: Dodd, 1935), 18.

Chapter 1 Start

1. James H. O'Keefe et al., "Potential Adverse Cardiovascular Effects From Excessive Endurance Exercise," *Mayo Clinic Proceedings*, 87, no 6 (June 2012): 587-595, doi: 10.1016/j.mayocp.2012.04.005.

2. Lisa Freedman, "Bizarre Facts About Ultramarathoning," *Men's Fitness*, accessed June 20, 2014, http://www.mensfitness.com/life/sports/bizarre-facts-about-ultramarathoning.

3. "About the Trail," *Illinois Prairie Path*, accessed January 4, 2015, http://www.ipp.org/about-the-trail.

Chapter 2 Train

1. Jon Erdman, "NOAA: Winter 2013-2014 Among Coldest on Record in Midwest; Driest, Warmest in Southwest," *The Weather Channel*, accessed June 12, 2014, http://www.weather.com/news/news/winter-ncdc-state-climate-report-2013-2014-20140313.

2. "Perspectives: Door County News, Arts, and Entertainment," *Door County Pulse*, (Door County, WI), December 20, 2013.

3. "Wisconsin State Park System: Peninsula State Park," *Wisconsin Department of Natural Resources*, accessed January 4, 2015, http://dnr.wi.gov/topic/parks/name/peninsula.

4. Reuters, "Can Exercise Detox Your Body? It's Not about the Sweat," *TODAY Health & Wellness* (2012), accessed July 10, 2014, http://www.today.com/health/can-exercise-detox-your-body-its-not-about-sweat-1C7634616.

5. *Half Marathon Coach*, Mobile application software, MapMyFITNESS Inc, version 2.0, accessed May 2011, https://itunes.apple.com/us/genre/ios/id36?mt=8.

Chapter 3 Breath

1. "Meditation: Take a Stress-Reduction Break Wherever You Are," *Mayo Clinic*, accessed July 20, 2014, http://www.mayoclinic.org/tests-procedures/meditation/in-depth/meditation/art-20045858.

2. "Stress Management: Relaxation Techniques; Try These Steps to Reduce Stress," *Mayo Clinic,* accessed July 20, 2014, http://www.mayoclinic.org/healthy-living/stress-management/in-depth/relaxation-technique/art-20045368?pg=2.

Chapter 4 Heal

1. *Wikipedia*, s.v. "methicillin-resistant Staphylococcus aureus (MRSA)," accessed September 24, 2014, http://en.wikipedia.org/wiki/Methicillin-resistant_Staphylococcus_aureus.

2. Sidewalk Prophets, "Keep Making Me," in *Live Like That,* Fervent Records, 2012, compact disc.

Chapter 5 Pace

1. James MacDonald, "Don't Shrink God" (sermon, Harvest Bible Chapel, Rolling Meadows, IL, August 16, 2014).

2. Steve Jobs, "Stanford Address" (graduation speech, Stanford University, Palo Alto, CA, June 14, 2005).

3. *Door County Bakery,* accessed September 20, 2014, http://www.doorcountybakery.com.

Chapter 6 Gear

1. Sungho Lee, *Flashcard Elite: Proven Memory Algorithm for Flashcards*, Mobile application software, version 1.2.6, accessed November 4, 2013, www.flashcardelite.com.

2. Peter Jensen, *Bible Memory–to God Be the Glory*, Mobile application software, version 1.1.1, accessed October 16, 2014, BibleMemorApp@gmail.com.

3. *Wikipedia*, s.v "canonical hours," accessed July 15, 2014, http://en.wikipedia.org/wiki/Canonical_hours.

4. *Wikipedia*, s.v. "Revised Common Lectionary," accessed July 15, 2014, http://en.wikipedia.org/wiki/Revised_Common_Lectionary.

5. *Wikipedia*, s.v. "Book of Common Prayer," accessed July 15, 2014, http://en.wikipedia.org/wiki/Book_of_Common_Prayer.

6. Steven Romej, *Chronicle for iPhone*, Mobile application software, version 1.4.1, accessed January 2011, www.slidetorock.com.

Chapter 7 Race

1. *Wikipedia*, s.v. "Jeff Galloway," June 6, 2014, http://en.wikipedia.org/wiki/Jeff_Galloway.

Chapter 8 Recover

1. Swenson, 91-92.

2. "Greens N Grains Natural Foods Market & Café: About" *Greens N Grains Natural Foods Market Café*, accessed November 25, 2014, http://www.greens-n-grains.com.

3. "Instructors: Kathy Navis," *Junction Center Yoga Studio*, accessed November 25, 2014, http://www.junctioncenteryoga.com.

4. "Videos," *Harvest Bible Chapel*, accessed November 25, 2014, http://www.harvestbiblechapel.org/10780/content/content_id/312160/Videos.

5. Galatians 5:22–23 (NIV).

Chapter 9 Finish
1. *Dictionary.com*, s.v. "abide," accessed August 25, 2014, Dictionary.comhttp://dictionary.reference.com/browse/abide.
2. "Chicago Half Marathon & Hyundai Hope On Wheels 5K," *Chicago Half Marathon*, accessed September 25, 2014, http://www.chicagohalfmarathon.com.
3. "About Mitchell Swaback Charities," *Harvest Compassion Center: Mitchell Swaback Charities*, accessed September 27, 2014, http://www.mitchellswabackcharities.org.
4. "Act Like Men Conference," (Indiana Convention Center, Indianapolis, IN, November 8, 2013), http://actlikemen.com.
5. Matthew 25:21a (NIV).
6. *Wikipedia*, s.v. "Mount Moran," accessed December 10, 2014, http://en.wikipedia.org/wiki/Mount_Moran.
7. "Longs Peak," *National Parks Service*, accessed January 3, 2015, http://www.nps.gov/romo/planyourvisit/longspeak.htm.

CPSIA information can be obtained at www.ICGtesting.com
Printed in the USA
LVOW11s0408130416

483321LV00001B/1/P